TEACHING BOYS AND YOUNG MEN OF COLOR:

A GUIDEBOOK

M
P
MONTEZUMA
PUBLISHING

Montezuma Publishing
San Diego, CA

Please direct comments regarding this resource to:

Montezuma Publishing
Aztec Shops Ltd.
San Diego State University
San Diego, CA 92182-1701
619-594-7552
Email: Montezuma@aztecmail.com
Website: www.montezumapublishing.com

This guidebook serves as a training resource for the Center for Organizational Responsibility and Advancement (CORA).

Center for Organizational Responsibility and Advancement (CORA)
6225 Hobart Street
San Diego, California 92115

Email: admin@coralearning.org
Website: www.coralearning.org
Training Website: www.training.coralearning.org

First published in the United States of America by
Lawndale Hill Publishing, 2016

ISBN (Print) – 978-0-7442-3471-8
ISBN (e-Book) – 978-0-7442-3472-5

Production Credits
Production mastering by: Shaila Mulholland, PhD
Quality Control: Marissa Vasquez Urias, EdD and Bridget Herrin, EdD
Cover design: Lia Dearborn
Cover photo: Close Up of Boys in Library©iStockphoto/Susan Chiang

TABLE OF CONTENTS

REVIEW CREDITS

This publication was peer-reviewed by:

Fred A. Bonner II, EdD

Rikesha L. Fry Brown, PhD

Idara R. Essien, PhD

Alonzo A. Flowers, PhD

Juan Carlos Gonzalez, PhD

John D. Harrison, PhD

Adriel A. Hilton, PhD

Rebecca A. Neal, PhD

Christopher B. Newman, PhD

Marissa Vasquez Urias, EdD

DEDICATION

This book is dedicated to the educators who advocate, support, and love our boys and young men of color.

This book is also dedicated to our sons, J. Luke Wood Jr. and A. J. Harris who serve as the motivation for our work on males of color in education.

ACKNOWLEDGMENTS

The authors of this guidebook would like to acknowledge the 216 classroom teachers who participated in this study. Their insights, recommendations, and passion were critical to the completion of this volume. The authors would also like to acknowledge the Minority Male Community College Collaborative (M2C3) research team, who have helped to hone ideas and concepts encapsulated in this book. They include: Nexi Delgado, Soua Xiong, Angelica Palacios, Melissa Vang, Stephanie Mathew, Jamal Mazyck, Vannessa Falcon, Annan Gaggi, and Dr. Marissa Vasquez Urias. In addition, the authors are appreciate of the contributions and feedback of Dr. Idara R. Essien on previous iterations of this document.

PREFACE

A Clarion Call for Action

During his second term in Office, President Barack Obama established the My Brother's Keeper (MBK) initiative. The initiative was designed to "address persistent opportunity gaps faced by boys and young men of color" (White House, 2014, para. 1). In partnership with major philanthropic organizations, MBK has advanced promising practices, policy, and program evaluation to improve the lives of boys, young men, and men of color in society. In particular, MBK established six milestones (or areas of intervention) and four of these milestones focus specifically on enhancing male success in education. These target areas emphasize improving the readiness of children for early schooling experiences, reading proficiency at grade-level, high school graduation rates, and completion of post-secondary certificates and degrees.

These MBK emphases highlight the critical role that education has in determining life outcomes in employment, criminal justice, and health care. Education has long been heralded as a primary venue for upward social and economic mobility for communities of color. As adeptly stated by Malcolm X in 1964: "Education is an important element in the struggle for human rights...education is our passport to the future, for tomorrow belongs only to the people who prepare for it today." MBK has helped to advance national dialogue on the experience and outcomes of males of color in education. The highest office in the land has now set the stage for efforts across the nation; in essence, providing support for educators to focus on real issues affecting student success and to respond with practical interventions to redress evident disparities. There is a common concern for the moral health of our educational system and nation, which is guilty of an accumulation of transgressions against Black and Latino boys, young men, and men. We come to this conversation today at what may be the turn of the tide, a critical point where concern and action align in ways that allow educators to challenge the status quo and advance outcomes for these males.

There is a common concern for the moral health of our educational system and nation, which is guilty of an accumulation of transgressions against Black and Latino boys, young men, and men.

This volume was inspired by President Obama's national clarion call for action and is grounded in years of research that we and our colleagues have engaged in on males of color in education. Our goal here is to make meaningful contributions to practice by better preparing educators to work with a student population that is misunderstood and all too often mis-educated. There are many teachers with good hearts and righteous intentions who struggle to facilitate success for males of color, particularly for Black and Latino boys and young men. We believe that this is a result of teacher preparation programs that inadequately prepare teachers and classroom aids to effectively educate this population.

Too often, when educators produce poor student outcomes for males of color, the reactionary response is to blame the students, their families, and their communities for inadequate outcomes. However, we have learned through our research that there are teachers that have had great success in educating this population. Their success suggests that the deficit reactionary response is misplaced; rather, the success of boys and young men of color in education is largely within the hands of the educators who work with them. Specifically, there are strategies that can be effectively employed to build relationships and educate this population. These strategies, and the base understanding of why they are integral to success, are not sufficiently present in the educational experiences of these students. As such, the insights from teachers who have experienced success with boys and young men of color served as the guiding framework for this volume.

This book can serve as a beneficial guide for all educators who work with boys and young men of color in schools. This includes classroom aids, teachers, counselors, school psychologists, community educators, and administrators. We also believe that all individuals working in schools have a responsibility for supporting the learning and development of students. As such, custodians, bus drivers, cafeteria staff, classroom volunteers and other personnel may find the information contained in the volume to be value added. In addition, parents, guardians, and family members may also find information in this guidebook that can provide insight for them on how they can better advocate for and support their sons. That being said, the recommendations for practice offered here focus on a learning experience that is most often facilitated by classroom teachers. Teachers are among those school professionals who are most readily positioned to effect change for boys and young men of color. Primarily, this is due to learning structures that enable teachers to interact with students more often than other school educators.

Teachers are among those school professionals who are most readily positioned to effect change for boys and young men of color.

The recommendations for practice highlighted in this guidebook were derived from several key sources. First, we reviewed extant research on boys and young men of color in education. While works in numerous sub-fields were examined, we were most deeply engaged with writings on culturally relevant pedagogy, critical race theory, the social construction of identity, healthy school climates, as well as equity-mindedness and institutional responsibility. Second, we leveraged applicable concepts and theories from our own extensive scholarship on teaching and learning for males of color in education. This work has chiefly examined the educational realities of Black, Latino, Native American, Southeast Asian, and Pacific Islander men during their transitions from high school to college and in post-secondary education. A significant component of this work is derived from two projects with *faculty leaders* in community colleges. These projects identified faculty who had been successful in serving men from historically underrepresented and underserved groups and elicited their perspectives on promising teaching and learning strategies through interviews and narratives (Wood, Harris III, & White, 2015).

Finally, the vast majority of what is presented in this volume is directly informed from a recently concluded national study of teachers who had a proven record of success in teaching Black and Latino boys and young men in preK-12 education (aka "exemplar teachers"). Teachers who had taught for at least three years and had a demonstrated track record of success in teaching males of color based on measurable outcomes were nominated by their school principals to participate in this study. A total of 216 teachers participated in this study, providing narratives of their successes in educating Black and Latino males in response to structured prompts. These teachers were recruited from six states that had the nation's highest concentration of populations of color, including: California, Florida, Georgia, New York, North Carolina, and Texas. These states were also recognized for having extensive geographic, political, and cultural diversity; thereby increasing the usefulness of the strategies offered beyond the targeted states. Moreover, the majority of the teachers who participated in this study did not share the same racial and/or gender background of the students. These teachers often contextualized their comments from this vantage, with statements beginning with "As a White female, I have found..." or "Being a Black female, I engage..."

What is espoused herein may be generally recognized as simply 'good teaching'...What makes these strategies special, is that they have an intensified benefit on the teaching and learning enterprise for boys and young men of color.

The recommendations for practice derived from the study with successful educators study have illuminated several points. In the study, 72% of the teachers agreed that the teaching and learning experience of boys and young men of color required revised or enhanced strategies. But, what is espoused herein may be generally recognized as simply *good teaching*. That being said, the educators in the study asserted that these necessary strategies are often not used in the schooling experiences of males of color. The strategies advocated in this volume work with all students, regardless of their background. What makes these strategies special is that they have an intensified benefit on the teaching and learning enterprise for boys and young men of color. Moreover, the strategies offered can also serve to advance educational outcomes for other student groups who have been historically undersupported and underserved in education. Again, what makes the use of the offered strategies so critical is their intensified benefit for males of color. This is due to the role of external life pressures, male gender-role socialization, racial stereotypes, under-exposure to effective preparation experiences, and several other factors. These factors and the need to improve educational outcomes for Black and

Latino males (as well as for other boys and young men of color) are addressed extensively in Chapter 1.

Recommendations offered in this volume are derived from teachers across grade levels and address topics relevant to boys and young men. As expected, not all recommendations offered will be transferrable across grade level, with some strategies more appropriate for early childhood education, and others having more utility for high schoolers. Nevertheless, principles embodied within these strategies (e.g., patience, respect, caring) will have utility throughout the educational pipeline. Moreover, given the incredible diversity within Black and Latino communities, readers should know that some recommendations will be more applicable to the populations they work with than others. Thus, educators are encouraged to glean strategies that are directly useful for their target populations as well as contemplate how principles most applicable to other grade levels can be actualized for target populations of interest.

One obvious limitation of this volume and the research presented herein is that it reports on the perspectives of *educators* working with males of color. The voices of boys and men of color in recommending strategies that benefit their success are critical to a holistic perspective of promising practices (see Howard, 2014). That being said, this study still represents a critical addition to the scholarly and practitioner literature, as it focuses on improving what is taking place, rather than on the challenges facing the educational success of Black and Latino males in education.

When reading this volume, we invite you to engage feelings of discomfort, angst, and even anger as critical moments where your growth can best occur. You may find that journaling about your learning, reactions to the material, disagreements, and areas of confirmation can best support the translation of the recommendations discussed in this guidebook into your own practice. Collective sense-making of this material in a professional learning community (PLC) or a small group of educators may also serve to provoke insights that can help to facilitate change in the teaching of boys and young men of color. Regardless of how you choose to engage this material, we thank you for embarking on a journey designed to improve the educational realities and life outcomes of our nation's boys and young men of color.

REFERENCES

Howard, T. C. (2014). *Black male(d): Peril and promise in the education of African American males.* New York, NY: Teachers College Press.

White House. (2014). My Brother's Keeper. Retrieved June 2, 2014, from http://www.whitehouse.gov/my-brothers-keeper

Wood, J. L., Harris III, F., & White, K. (2015). *Teaching men of color in the community college: A guidebook.* San Diego, CA: Montezuma.

CHAPTER 1

A Contextual Overview of Challenges

In this chapter, we will provide a foundation for understanding why the teaching and learning practices offered in this volume are critical to success for males of color. We do so by highlighting some of the outcome disparities experienced by Black and Latino males that have served as motivation for the national conversation on these students. Also examined are perspectives for making sense of these outcomes and designing productive responses to identified breakdowns.

Advancing the success of boys and young men of color is a topic regularly addressed by scholars and practitioners alike. Largely, this is due to deleterious outcomes experienced by Black and Latino males in education. The challenges facing these students are evident early on (Howard, 2014; Noguera, 2003; Saenz & Ponjuan, 2009; Seven Centers Report, 2014). Reading is a critical determinant of future success in school, serving as the building block for learning in all academic disciplines. However, data from the National Assessment of Educational Progress (NAEP, 2013) demonstrated that only 14% and 18% of Black and Latino boys in fourth grade were at or above proficient in reading. These rates are dwarfed by that of their White and Asian male peers, who read at rates roughly three times higher at 41% and 47%, respectively. Similarly, trends in fourth grade mathematics demonstrate comparable differences, with only 18% of Black boys who were at or above proficient in math. This rate is in comparison to math proficiency rates of 55% and 64% for White and Asian boys. While Latino boys fare better in math with 28% proficiency than they do in reading, their success is marginal at best in comparison to their White and Asian peers.

Reading is a critical determinant of future success in school, serving as the building block for learning in all academic disciplines.

Unfortunately, patterns evidenced in fourth grade do not improve at subsequent levels of education. Eighth grade proficiency rates in math and reading have motivated the widely discussed opportunity gaps for these males. For example, by eighth grade, math and reading scores for Black males demonstrate disastrously low levels of proficiency, at 13% and 12%. Moreover, Latino male success in these same fields is also concerning, at 21% and 17% for math and reading. These percentages for historically undersupported males of color serve as an indictment to an educational system that produces significantly higher levels of success for White and Asian males. For example, 45% and 59% of White and Asian males will be at proficient or above in math and 38% and 43% in reading (NAEP, 2013). Given these proficiency trends, it is not surprising that Black and Latino males are underrepresented in advanced schooling experiences (e.g., gifted education, advanced placement, honors, dual enrollment, International Baccalaureate).

Only 52% and 58% of Black and Latino males graduated from high school in four years.

The manifold effects of outcome challenges at earlier levels of education are extended to high school graduation rates for young men of color. According to the Schott Foundation (2012), only 52% and 58% of Black and Latino males graduated from high school in four years. In stark contrast, 78% of White males completed high school in the same time frame. However, there is wide variation across states and districts, with some locales performing at even lower levels of success. For example, only 38% of Black males and 46% of Latino males graduated from high school in the District of Columbia. Moreover, success rates for both Black and Latino males in New York mark in at only 37%. In fact, the Schott Foundation has identified numerous states with Black and Latino graduation rates below 60%, such as Alabama, Colorado, Connecticut, Delaware, Florida, Georgia, Michigan, Mississippi, and South Carolina.

Black and Latino boys and young men are significantly more likely to be subjected to exclusionary discipline than their peers.

One rationale for disparate success outcomes for these males can be attributed to the disciplinary practices used on them. Black and Latino boys and young men are significantly more likely to be subjected to exclusionary discipline than their peers (Lewis, Butler, Bonner II, & Joubert, 2010). Exclusionary discipline refers to disciplinary practices that remove them for learning environments, thereby, restricting them from learning opportunities necessary for their success. The implementation of exclusionary discipline begins early on, with Black children accounting for 42% of all preschoolers who are suspended one time and 48% of those suspended more than once, despite representing only 18% of the preschool population (AFT, 2015).

This pattern continues into K-12 schooling, as 15% of Black males were the recipients of out-of-school suspensions, compared to only 5% of White males (Schott Foundation, 2015). Comparatively, Latino male out-of-school suspension rates are at 7%. However, like disparities evident across states in graduation data, certain states have even more egregious suspension levels. For example, 23% of Black boys received out-of-school suspensions in the state of Florida, in comparison to 9% of White males and 10% of Latino males. Some locales have even more striking rates, with Polk County in Florida and St. Louis Missouri giving out-of-school suspensions to 40% of their Black males. Similar to suspension patterns, the expulsion rate for Black males is nearly three times higher than that of White males. Nationally, 0.61% of Black males were expelled from school, compared with 0.29% of Latino males and 0.21% of White males. That being said, the nation's highest expulsion rate belongs to Oklahoma, where 3.7% of Black males were expelled, with 1.3% and 0.7% of Latino and White males receiving expulsions in that state (Schott Foundation, 2015).

While subject to high out-of-school suspension rates and expulsions, boys and young men of color are also more likely to be overrepresented in special education. Although special education can serve as an important intervention and support site for students in need of individualized resources, procedures, and practices that advance their learning, it can also serve as a "dumping" ground for students who teachers have struggled with. While it is certainly true that boys account for the lion's share of all students in special education, at 67%, Black and Latino boys account for nearly 80% of all boys in special education (Ricks, 2013).

Boys of color are egregiously overrepresented among students with mental retarded and emotionally disturbed classifications.

Boys of color are egregiously overrepresented among students with mental retarded and emotionally disturbed classifications. For instance, while Black males account for only 9% of the student population, they are significantly over classified as mentally retarded, comprising 20% of all students labeled with this designation (National Education Association, 2011). As a result, they are 2.5 times more likely than their peers to be designated by their schools as mentally retarded (Council for Greater City Schools, 2010). However, disproportionate classifications are not limited to this designation, Black males are also disproportionately classified as emotionally disturbed at 21% (Smith, 2004).

Overrepresentation in special education in general, and in these classifications in particular, illuminate the role of stereotypes, systemic breakdowns, and inadequate educator preparation in fostering disparate outcomes for Black and Latino males. Furthermore, there is a connection here with the high percentage of young men and men of color involved in the juvenile justice and criminal justice systems. Many youth and adults in these systems are currently or were formerly in special education. For example, 28% of Latino prisoners and 26% of Black prisoners have at least one disability (Bureau of Justice Statistics, 2015).

One in every three Black men and one of our every six Latino men can expect to be imprisoned at some point in their lifetime.

Latino males are twice as likely as their White male peers and six times more likely than their Asian counterparts to be in incarcerated in a juvenile justice facility (Bureau of Justice Statistics, 2015). Similarly, Black males are 4.5 times more likely than their White peers and 15 times more likely than their Asian peers to be in a juvenile facility. These striking disparities only increase after they become adults, where one in nine Black men and one in 24 Latino men between the ages of 20 to 24 will be incarcerated. These rates are juxtaposed with only one in 60 White men in the same age range who are incarcerated (Pew, 2008). In fact, one in every three Black men and one of every six Latino men can expect to be imprisoned at some point in their lifetime (Amurao, 2012; Center for American Progress, 2012). Being incarcerated can also have intergenerational effects of youth. For example, research from Roettger and Swisher (2011) found that there is a significantly higher probability of juvenile delinquency when a father has been incarcerated.

MAKING SENSE OF THESE OUTCOMES

These aforementioned data serve as fodder for the national dialogue on the success of boys and young men of color. Clearly, educational institutions struggle to provide outcomes for males of color that are in line with those experienced by their peers. According to W. Edward Deming and Paul Bataldon "every system is perfectly designed to achieve the results it gets". Bringing this thinking and critical perspective down to a more personal level helps to demonstrate the role that educators have as parts of the system. In reality, every district, every school, and every classroom are all perfectly designed to achieve the results that they get. From this perspective, the widespread challenges facing Black and Latino males in the educational system are a byproduct of the system itself. As part of this system, all educators have some culpability in the results produced by the system.

Every district, every school, and every classroom are all perfectly designed to achieve the results that they get.

Many educators do not make sense of inadequate educational outcomes for boys and young men of color from this perspective. Instead, they may respond to data presented in this chapter by asking, "What is wrong with these boys? Why aren't they doing what it takes for them to be successful?" This sensemaking is referred to as deficit framing (see Bensimon, 2005). Deficit framing is the predominant way of viewing student success, seeing breakdowns as a function of inadequacies in the students, their families, and their communities. Deficit perspectives focus on students' lack of preparation, poor academic habits, not caring about education, or having insufficient support from family. Collectively, these perspectives perceive inadequate student success as being attributable to a *culture of disadvantage*.

We acknowledge that students and their families serve as a critical component of the educational process. In tandem with educators, they share responsibility for breakdowns in learning and development; nevertheless, the deficit frame offers very little in terms of changing the widespread challenges facing the teaching and learning enterprise for Black and Latino males. Certainly, any concerted action to change current educational outcomes that is rooted in this perspective will only shift the focus of responsibility away from educators. Rather, educators should focus their energies on improving their practice because this is what is within their realm of influence and control. As adeptly noted by Harris III, Bensimon, and Bishop (2010), "It is futile to dwell on students' past experiences. It is also harmful if inequalities are rationalized as beyond the control of practitioners. We must focus on what *is* within the control of educators in terms of changing their own practices to meet the needs and circumstances" (p. 280) of boys and young men of color.

Educators should focus their energies on improving factors their practice because this is what is within their realm of influence and control.

With this perspective in mind, we encourage educators to embrace a more productive viewpoint that is juxtaposed to the deficit frame. Bensimon (2005) argues that educators should employ an equity frame. An equity frame rationalizes disparate outcomes as a function of educational institutions (e.g., programs, policies, practices, curriculum, structures) and their agents (e.g., teachers, counselors, classroom aids). Breakdowns in student performance are then attributed to breakdowns in the institutions where they are educated. From this vantage point, sensemaking of disparities begins with questions such as "what are *we* doing or not doing as a district or school that results in our Black and Latino boys not doing as well as they should?" Even more specifically, teachers can also ask, "What am I doing or not doing in my classroom that is resulting or continuing educational disparities for my boys of color?" This perspective will result in more productive interventions that focus on areas that are within the control of education, such as teaching practices, curricular design, relationships with students and their families, and assessment of one's practice. The practices that are produced from this perspective must also take into account the unique attributes and identities of boys and young men of color, topics that are addressed in the next chapter.

REFERENCES

AFT. (2015). *Reclaiming the promise of racial equity in education, economics, and our criminal justice system. A report of the American Federal of Teachers Racial Equity Taskforce.* Washington, DC: American Federation of Teachers.

Amurao, C. (2012). *Fact sheet: How bad is the school-to-prison pipeline?* Arlington, VA: KPBS.

Bensimon, E. M. (2005). Closing the achievement gap in higher education: An organizational learning perspective. *New Directions for Higher Education, 131,* 99-111.

Bureau of Justice Statistics. (2015, December 14). *About a third of prison and jail inmates reported a disability in 2011-2012.* Washington, DC: Author.

Center for American Progress. (2012). *The top 10 most startling facts about people of color and criminal justice in the United states: A look at the racial disparities inherent in our nation's criminal-justice system.* Washington, DC: Author.

Council for Greater City Schools. (2010). *A call for change: The social and educational factors contributing to the outcomes of Black males in urban schools.* Washington, DC: Author.

Harris III, F., Bensimon, E. M., & Bishop, R. (2010). The Equity Scorecard: A process for building institutional capacity to educate young men of color. In C. Edley, Jr. & J. Ruiz de Velasco (Eds.), *Changing places: How communities will improve the health of boys of color* (pp. 277-308). Berkeley, CA: University of California Press.

Howard, T. C. (2014). *Black male(d): Peril and promise in the education of African American males.* New York, NY: Teachers College Press.

Lewis, C. W., Butler, B. R., Bonner III, F. A., & Joubert, M. (2010). African American male discipline patterns and school district responses resulting impact on academic achievement: Implications for urban educators and policy makers. *Journal of African American Males in Education, 1*(1), 7-25.

NAEP. (2013). *U.S. Department of Education, Institute of Education Sciences, National Assessment of Educational Progress (NAEP), 2013 Mathematics and Reading Assessment.* Washington, DC: National Center for Education Statistics.

National Education Association. (2011, February). *Race against time: Educating Black boys.* Washington, DC: Author.

Noguera, P. A. (2003). The trouble with Black boys: The role and influence of environmental and cultural factors on the academic performance of African American males. *Urban Education, 38*(4), 431-459.

Pew Foundation. (2008). *One in 100: Behind bars in America 2008.* Washington, DC: Author.

Ricks, D. (2013). *Educating boys for success: Are today's classrooms biased against boys?* Washington, DC: National Education Association.

Roettger, M. E., & Swisher, R. R. (2011). Associations of fathers' history of incarceration with sons' delinquency and arrest among Black, White, and Hispanic males in the United States. *Criminology, 49*(4), 1109-1147.

Saenz, V.B., & Ponjuan, L. (2009). The vanishing Latino male in higher education. *Journal of Hispanic Higher Education, 8*(1), 54-89.

Schott Foundation. (2012). *The urgency of now: The Schott 50 state report on public education and Black males.* Cambridge, MA: Author.

Schott Foundation. (2015). *Black lives matter: The Schott 50 state report on public education and Black males.* Cambridge, MA: Author.

Seven Centers Report. (2014). Advancing *the* success *of* boys *and* men *of* color: *Recommendations for policy makers.* Contributions from The Center for the Study of Race and Equity in Education, Minority Male Community College Collaborative, Morehouse Research Institute, Project MALES and the Texas Education Consortium for Male Students of Color, Todd Anthony Bell National Resource Center on the African American Male, Black Male Institute, Wisconsin's Equity and Inclusion Laboratory. San Diego, CA: Printing Office.

Smith, R. (2004, January 20). *Saving Black boys.* Washington, DC: The American Prospect.

CHAPTER 2

Factors Necessitating Enhanced Teaching Practice

This chapter highlights three interrelated areas that necessitate an enhanced teaching and learning experience for boys and young men of color. These areas include: external life pressures, racial-gender stereotypes, and male gender-role socialization.

Boys and young men of color have unique experiences that must be taken into account by educators. The study respondents identified common challenges facing Black and Latino males in education that require revised or enhanced teaching strategies. These issues encompass pressures in students' home lives and communities, racial-gender stereotypes, and male gender-role socialization. That being said, *the* most common barrier identified by study respondents focuses on the preparation of educators to work with Black and Latino males. They noted that teachers often struggle to build rapport, maintain high expectations for students' performance, convey content in culturally relevant ways, and build connections with students. These are viewed as salient barriers that produce disparate experiences for boys and young men of color in comparison to their peers. Thus, while we address mediating barriers here, it should be noted that the respondents, as well as extensive research, demonstrate that these factors have less of an effect on student success than the relationships and teaching practices employed by educators. As such, from an institutional responsibility perspective, these factors serve to inform practices that should take place, rather than shift the onus of student success on factors outside the control of educators.

The most common barrier identified by study respondents focuses on the preparation of educators to work with Black and Latino males.

EXTERNAL LIFE PRESSURES

There are numerous barriers that are often, but not always, faced by boys and young men of color. Some of these barriers are referred to as external life pressures, or factors that occur outside of school but influence student success in school. These barriers are typically a function of structural disparities and racism that disproportionately disadvantage communities of color. A number of the educators with a proven record of success in teaching boys and young men of color detailed the complex array of external life pressures facing their students. These factors ranged from hunger and unhealthy eating, documentation status, transportation concerns, inadequate technology at home, and trauma. An understanding of these pressures is necessary for educators to effectively empower students to gain critical agency in their own lives.

Most commonly, these educators identified poverty as one pervasive challenge facing these males. According to the U.S. Census Bureau (2014), many children of color are exposed to poverty. For instance, 10.7% of White children are raised in poverty, compared to 30.4% of Latino children and 38.3% of Black children who are raised in poverty. A 2015 report by My Brother's Keeper (2015) noted that "living in poverty means that parents must spend time and cognitive resources dealing with its many impacts, time and emotional energy that parents not living in poverty can spend in other ways, including on their children" (p. 7).

Black and Latino children are five to six times more likely to live in communities with concentrated poverty.

Some of these impacts may be even more acute based on varying degrees of poverty. Of the children in poverty, federal government data indicates that 52.5% of Black children and 42.7% of Latino children are living in *extreme* poverty (U.S. Census Bureau, 2013). Individual income disparities notwithstanding, it should also be noted that Black and Latino children are five to six times more likely to live in communities with concentrated poverty (National Kids Count, 2013a). This means that many of these students experience poverty on a micro-family level and at the community level. As such, it should not be surprising that Black and Latino children represent 58.3% of children in Title I schools (National Kids Count, 2015b).

Another common challenge experienced by Black and Latino children is that the communities they live in are also exposed to greater levels of safety concerns and crime. Unfortunately, 23% of Latino and Black children live in neighborhoods that are classified as being unsafe (National Kids Count, 2015c). Unsafe neighborhoods can influence school attendance. For example, a 2013 report from ETS indicated that young Black men in high school were two times more likely than

White students to attribute not attending school to feeling unsafe in either traveling to and from school or feeling unsafe being at school (ETS, 2013). Clearly, this is a critical point to consider as safety has long been recognized as a core need that is necessary for the development of emotional bonds, a sense of belonging, self-esteem, and fulfillment (Maslow, 1943).

Safety has long been recognized as a core need that is necessary for the development of emotional bonds, a sense of belonging, self-esteem, and fulfillment.

Given such external challenges, exposure to stressful events is also a common experience within communities of color. Stressful life events can include: financial hardship, divorce in the family, death of a parent, incarceration of a parent, violence in the family or neighborhood, living with an individual who is either suicidal or mentally ill, racial bias, or living with an individual struggling with substance abuse issues. A noticeable percentage of Black and Latino children are exposed to these conditions. In fact, 21% of Latino children and 31% of Black children experienced two or more stressful life events (National Kids Count, 2015d). Altogether, the cumulative effect of these events over time can inhibit success in education and other aspects of their lives. Furthermore, these stressful events do not decrease over time into adulthood, as research from Wood, Harris III and White (2015) demonstrates that Black and Latino college men experience four to five major stressful life events in a two-year time frame.

Finally, we would be remiss if we did not mention the role of family structure as being an external pressure. Some educators in the study noted that boys and young men of color are adversely affected by disintegrated families. Poverty, stress, generational racism, and high rates of incarceration among men of color have wreaked havoc on families of color. The vast majority, 67% of Black children are raised in single-parent families. Moreover, in a high percentage of these families, the father is not the primary caregiver or has negligible involvement. Regardless of parentage, the development of a healthy masculine identity is facilitated by positive male role models who can help dispel myths about gender-roles and masculinity. This challenge is endemic to Latino communities as well, where 42% come from single parent homes (National Kids Count, 2015e). Unfortunately, research has shown that single mothers are often exposed to challenges that can complicate childrearing, including: income challenges, unemployment, underemployment, depression, anxiety, and stress (Atkins, 2015; Mendenhall, Bowman, & Zhang, 2013). This is not to say that single parent families are incapable of raising healthy, productive, and academically successful young men. Many single parents, particularly single mothers, aunties, and grandmothers, have done an exemplary job in raising their sons. It is clear that when single parents provide an affirming environment within a supportive-loving community, their children will excel.

RACIAL-GENDER STEREOTYPES

Teachers with a proven record of success in working with males of color identified racism and stereotypes as being a central challenge facing this population. Daily encounters with racism remain a central element of the Black and Latino male experience. These encounters range from overt to subtle racialized encounters. The majority of such experiences are subtle in nature, being the derivative of unconscious bias that occurs in wider society and in schools. An awareness of common stereotypes encountered by these males is necessary for building environments that aggressively dispel myths and build environments of parity.

Daily encounters with racism remain a central element of the Black and Latino male experience. These encounters range from overt to subtle racialized encounters.

Over the past decade, media have covered numerous high profile slayings of young men and men of color. Many of these slayings took place at the hands of people in positions of power and perceived power. Names such as Trayvon Martin, Michael Brown, Tamir Rice, Freddie Gray, Michael Brown, Eric Garner, Jordan Davis, Oscar Grant III and Amadou Diallo have been widely cited as examples of how men of color are criminalized and then systematically targeted. These instances and others have served as the impetus for national dialogue surrounding police brutality and vigilantism (Wood et al., 2015). Regardless of the specific circumstances of each case, collectively they illuminate a disconcerting pattern that males of color are perceived as criminals and, thus, deserve to be treated more violently than their White male counterparts. Given that the primary cases highlighted have focused on Black males, the injustices routinely experienced by the Latino community have not been widely chronicled in national media. That being said, both communities suffer from similar perceptions and challenges.

Unfortunately, there is no magic barrier that prevents racism and stereotypes from entering into school settings. Males of color are often perceived by educators as deviants, delinquents, and criminals.

Unfortunately, there is no magic barrier that prevents racism and stereotypes from entering into school settings. Males of color are often perceived by educators as deviants, delinquents, and criminals. These perceptions shape how educators interpret their actions and interact with them. These perceptions are fueled by negative depictions of males of color as murderers, gangsters, rapists, drug dealers, and womanizers (e.g., pimp, the Latin lover). As noted by Wood and Hilton (2013), media prevent males of color from being perceived as "good or righteous individuals, rendering them as morally ambiguous beings. More often, they are presented as the vision of evil, embodying the loss of American morality" (p. 14). Wood and Hilton concluded that perceptions of these men range from amoral to immoral and are a function of both their racial and gender identities. Coupled with hyper-masculine portrayals of physical prowess, dominance, and rage, it is not surprising that even the most socially conscious educator may have a deep-seated or unconscious fear of Black and Latino males. Criminalized viewpoints of males of color adversely influence how educators respond to them. The disproportionately high use of exclusionary discipline practices with boys of color is one indicative example of this perspective. Young men of color are significantly more likely than their male peers to be suspended and expelled from school for behaviors that are not treated as harshly when performed by White males (The Seven Centers Report, 2014).

Young men of color are significantly more likely than their male peers to be suspended and expelled from school, often for actions on par with that of other boys, but perceived very differently by educators.

In addition to being perceived as criminals, males of color are often portrayed as being academically inferior. For example, Latino males are stereotypically viewed as being unintelligent and having little personal drive (Hudley & Graham, 2001).

Such perceptions of inferiority may be even more pervasive about Latinos who are English Language Learners (ELL), due to commonly advanced nativist arguments. In particular, these arguments characterize Spanish speaking migrant workers as "lowly," "menial," and "left-overs." Huynh (2012) noted that Latino adolescents receive subtle messages that stereotype their abilities, where educators may be surprised about the intellectual capabilities. Huynh found that microaggressions towards Latinos was associated with greater levels of anxiety, stress, and anger.

Research on Black males has also found negative stereotypes about intelligence to be commonly held by educators (Allen, 2012; Howard, 2014; Wood, 2014). For example, Wood (2014) found that Black males were apprehensive to engage in classrooms for fear of being perceived by educators and peers as 'dumb', 'unintelligent', and 'stupid.' As a result, when they needed to ask a question in class or had insights to contribute to class discussions, they refrained from doing so in order to avoid offering statements that could validate negative perceptions about their abilities.

The confluence of the two predominant stereotypes about Black and Latino males in school, as criminal and unintelligent, are critical for understanding their experiences at the hands of teachers. Guided by this notion, Ladson-Billings (2011) articulated four ways in which Black males are engaged by educators. First, they are engaged from a *fear and control* paradigm. In this paradigm, Black males are perceived as criminals, deviants, and threats. Schools respond to this perception by trying to control their actions and behaviors. She described evidence of this by juxtaposing her observations between two schools, one predominantly White and the other predominantly Black. In the predominantly White school, students are able to roam freely through the hallways and to and from classes. In the predominantly Black school, movement was restricted, students were placed in uniforms, they had very structured ways in which they were to line up, and talking was prevented in normal social places, such as the hallways and in the cafeteria. She concluded that the primary function of the school was socializing students for prison rather than a productive life.

First, they are engaged from a fear and control paradigm. In this paradigm, Black males are perceived as criminals, deviants, and threats. Schools respond to this perception by trying to control their actions and behaviors.

Second, Ladson-Billings (2011) noted that they are viewed as *infantiles* and *criminalized*. She stated that Black boys between the ages of three and six are often viewed as being cute, but are rarely recognized as being intelligent. Some educators overly focus on their cute appearance, but this perception quickly fades by the time they reach eight or nine years of age. At this point, educators view and engage them as men through the lenses of fear and control. A difference in treatment between them and their male peers becomes more readily apparent. A non-Black boy who repeatedly gets out of his seat is asked nicely to sit down and to listen. However, when a Black boy does the same thing, the first offense can result in disciplinary action and being sent to the principal's office. Many of these sentiments were shared by the teachers in the study.

Our own observations as researchers of the male of color experience have illuminated similar findings. Anecdotally, we have seen preschool teachers create environments of love and affirmation to support socio-emotional growth among children. In these environments, children extend the love they receive from teachers to one another, through hugging and patting. These environments are critical to fostering a sense of belonging in school and healthy development. Yet, such actions pose a difficult double standard for boys of color. Specifically, young affectionate boys of color (e.g., huggers) soon have their actions labeled as hypersexual, even as early as kindergarten, particularly when innocuous embraces occur with girls of White ancestry.

MALE GENDER SOCIALIZATION

Too often, conversations on males of color in education ignore the critical role that gender has on the experience of this population. Male gender-role socialization has a critical influence on how boys of color are engaged by and interpret educational settings. Socialization during boyhood for manhood begins early on. Boys are given toys (e.g., trucks, blocks) and dressed in a manner which teaches them early on that being a man means to be tough, to restrict one's emotions, and to be aggressive. As noted by Hughes (2012), messages about being a boy or man are facilitated through imitation and reinforcement. Boys learn to imitate actions and behaviors by viewing activities engaged in by older boys. Reinforcement is extended through praise and criticism. Boys are praised for performing masculine scripts (e.g., being interested in sports, being physical) and criticized when they engage in actions seen as feminine. For example, boys are told not to cry because 'boys don't cry.' When hurt, they are told to 'man up' and 'buck up.' Very quickly, boys inculcate socially constructed perceptions of masculinity, and begin finding intrinsic worth and satisfaction when demonstrating gender-appropriate behaviors.

Reinforcement is extended through praise and criticism. Boys are praised for performing masculine scripts.

Gender roles are conveyed to boys from a variety of sources, including: family members, parents, male and female peers, and by schools (Flowers, 2015; Flowers & Banda, 2015; Harris & Harper, 2008). For example, in homes with both a female and male parent/guardian, boys witness gender roles play out in terms of financial contribution, household chores and duties, and decision-making. Even for boys who are not raised in such family structures, common presentations of families on television include a mother who has primary authority over raising children, cleaning, cooking, and other duties commonly associated with femininity. Similarly, fathers and father-like figures are portrayed as tough and domineering disciplinarians who are also primary breadwinners. Normative messages about gender expectations are learned through in-home and on-media portrayals of family life (Wood et al., 2015).

Harris III and Harper (2008) suggest that male gender-role socialization is fundamentally incompatible with success in school. They explicated critical ways that male socialization influences academic achievement for boys and young men, conveying school as a White feminine domain and avoiding help-seeking. For example, 75% of K-12 school teachers are White and female. Thus, the socialized structure of power in the classroom is one that is both White and feminine, making school a domain best suited for White females. Given that school is social coded as a feminine space, boys who engage in school, who are studious, and smart are often teased for being "squares," "sissys," "soft," and "punks." Similarly, as explicated in the previous section, pervasive racial stereotypes suggest that children of color are academically inferior. This notion, coupled with the demographic of teachers as predominantly White, creates a circumstance where school is perceived as a White domain. Therefore, to be successful in this domain, children of color must often act in defiance to social expectations.

Boys and young men of color may seemingly reject school in exchange for visage of 'coolness', as a means of achieving social acceptance.

For boys of color, the confluence of both gender and racial messages at school places them in double jeopardy. Education and social science scholars (e.g., Harris, Palmer, & Struve, 2011; Majors, 2001; Majors & Billson, 1992) have long argued that boys and young men of color may seemingly reject school in exchange for visage of 'coolness,' as a means of achieving social acceptance. As noted by Jackson and Moore (2008), young boys' desire to be viewed as "cool" "encourage[s] behaviors that devalue academic achievement and express educational aspiration while condoning activities and relationships that rebuff traditional standards of academic success" (p. 849). In middle and high school, boys of color often adopt an identity that is rooted in being successful in sports and in gaining the attention of girls as a strategy to elevate their popularity and status within male peer groups. The desire to not be seen as studious was raised as a barrier among teachers in the study. Specifically, teacher participants stated: "Hispanic boys have a stigma about being 'smart'"; "Often, I have encountered their reticence to be seen as academically successful. It's not okay, better to be seen as athletic or popular or anti-school," and "Young men of color tend to shy away from the perception that they are smart."

Moreover, research from Harris III and Harper (2008), Saenz and Ponjuan (2009) and other scholars found that males are socialized to avoid help-seeking in exchange for being self-reliant and achievement focused. Specifically, boys are taught that seeking help is a sign of weakness and inferiority, traits not indicative of manhood. This perception can have deleterious effects on success in school, as young men of color will be apprehensive to seek help from teachers, meet with school counselors, or ask peers for assistance for fear of being perceived as inferior. For males of color, avoidance of help-seeking must also be viewed through a racial lens. Given the predominant perceptions of students of color (particularly boys and young men of color) as unintelligent, the act of help-seeking produces potential interactions where stereotypes about them can be affirmed (Wood, 2014). Moreover, unconscious bias can create circumstances where teachers who desire to provide assistance can interact with students in ways that unintentionally disparages their abilities. Hereto, the confluence of racial and gender identities intensifies their reluctance to engage in academic environments.

Teachers with a proven record of success with boys and young men of color also noted that the learning structure in the classroom is one that does not serve boys well. Boys tend to be active, have short attention spans, and be hands-on. These are patterns of engagement that are socialized through the types of toys that are purchased (e.g., trains, trucks, blocks, construction toys, model kits, workbenches and tools), the aspects of play that are encouraged (e.g., rough and tumble play, vigorous activity), and through sports (Hughes, 2010). However, the manner in which learning is conducted in the classroom prioritizes developmental trajectories for girls. Teachers from the study noted that classrooms are often structured in a manner that restricts movement, requires focus on tasks for long periods of time, and teaching modalities that do not engage gross motor skills. As a result, the teachers overwhelmingly recommended revising all aspects of the learning process to more intentionally levy attributes and assets that are generally observed among boys and young men.

The manner in which learning is conducted in the classroom prioritizes developmental trajectories for girls.

BRAIN AND HORMONAL DEVELOPMENT

While many of the differences in learning between boys and girls are a result of gender socialization, there is also credible evidence to suggest that brain and hormonal differences influence school success as well. We were apprehensive to present information on these differences, as biological arguments have long been used to dehumanize and justify ill-treatment of society's disadvantaged. That being said, studies in neuroscience have revealed that hormone secretion plays a role in emotion regulation. Since emotions play a role in regulating what gets stored and recalled from memory (Bresciani Ludvik, 2015), it becomes more and more evident that certain differences in learning and development occur across sex. To be explicitly clear, we are referring only to sex differences influenced by hormone secretion, not racial differences. To date, there is no replicated study that suggests that there are any learning and development differences between races that could be attributed to any biological differences in hormonal secretions (Bresciani Ludvik, 2015). Moreover, it should be noted that not all boys experience the same developmental processes.

While many of the differences in learning between boys and girls are a result of gender socialization, there is also credible evidence to suggest that brain and hormonal differences influence school success as well.

Gurian and Stevens (2008) have noted that positron emission tomography (PET) scans and magnetic resonance imaging (MRI) machines have illuminated key sex differences that may contribute to learning variances between boys and girls. Here are some key findings from Gurian and Stevens (with comments from Brescian Ludvik in italics):

- **Physical Activity.** Boys learn less well than girls when inactive and deskbound and retain and recall content information far better when physically active. In fact, movement is critical to learning for the male brain. In later developmental stages of learning and development, activity has proven critical to fostering increased learning in both sexes. This *may* be a byproduct of dopamine levels in the bloodstream; *however, there is disagreement on this point among scholars. What is clear is that movement is good for facilitating learning.*

- **Tactile Learning.** Boys perform better when information is conveyed through sensory-tactile (touching) experiences than aurally (hearing). This is a result of differences in temporal lobe neural connectivity that facilitate listening and memory storing. *This may also be due to another rationale: movement helps boys connect with sensing and feeling, which may help better regulate emotion and attention to learn.*

- **Impulsivity.** Boys are more likely to make decisions that seem impulsive and self-determined. In certain learning environments impulsivity may be perceived as more beneficial than others, which may be a result of differences in activity in their frontal lobes and boys' ability to down-regulate the emotions that lead to impulsivity *or reduced awareness of choice.*

- **Competition and Aggression.** Boys tend to learn better through exercises that are more hierarchical, competitive and aggressive-nurturing in nature. They are also more likely to build bonds with others through such activities. This is a byproduct of hormonal differences in testosterone and vasopressin that regulate aggression, territoriality, and hierarchy *(related to attention and emotion regulation). However, it is critical to recognize that excessive levels of competition and aggression can be harmful as they may reinforce social* *norms and the neural connectivity associated with them (i.e., train the brain in unhealthy ways).*

- **Overstimulation.** The brains of young men can become overstimulated when multi-tasking or moving between tasks too quickly. Overstimulation can lead to frustration, and over-activating the same center in the brain where anger and aggression are centered. Thus, a connection between overstimulation and disciplinary problems (i.e., acting out) is believed to exist.

- **Recharging.** Boys brains need periods of time where they are not stimulated in order to recharge, this is referred to as the *rest state*. This occurs when shifting between activities and tasks. The rest state is *critical* to renewing and reorienting the male brain before engaging a new task. Unfortunately, this vital brain function can be interpreted as "zoning out", "falling asleep," or "disengagement."

- **Visual Aids and Objects.** Boys' brains perform best when they experience spatial-visual stimulation. Visual aids (e.g., diagrams, pictures, maps, making models, coloring, patterns). Moreover, their brains are also best stimulated when spatial-mechanical learning is employed with objects that can move through space (e.g., chess, learning board games, blocks).

The aforementioned areas demonstrate how a male brain is unique and the specific teaching methodologies that advance learning and development. Unfortunately, the current structure of learning environments in many schools does not support male brain learning. Moreover, "asking boys of color to suppress emotions and physical movement in their learning environment is unwise, at best. Emotions play a role in regulating what gets stored and recalled from memory. Movement has been shown to enhance the retaining and recalling of information. Asking boys of color to suppress emotions and stay still, without having given them any strategies to regulate attention and emotion can be incredibly oppressive" (Bresciani Ludvik, 2015). It should also be noted that many of the aforementioned areas of brain learning align with and are intensified by socialization processes that emphasize aggression, movement, competition, and physical activity. Neuroplasticity has evidence that what an individual focuses upon literally changes the structure and corresponding function of the brain (Bresciani Ludvik, 2016). Thus, appropriate socialization can support and extend male brain learning and development.

Many conventional male traits are pathologized when performed by boys of color.

In addition, it should be noted that many conventional male traits are pathologized when performed by boys of color. For example, a boy of color whose brain may be in *rest state* can be viewed as being uncaring and withdrawn; a boy of color who demonstrates aggression is perceived as being vile and criminal when other boys are seen as competitive; and boys of color who struggle to sit still in class are characterized as not willing to listen, overly fidgety, and even defiant. As such, different interpretations of normal sex-based actions are often interpreted very differently by teachers for boys of color in comparison to their peers.

REFERENCES

Allen, Q. (2012). "They think minority means lesser than": Black middle-class sons and fathers resisting microaggressions in the school. Urban Education, 48(2), 171-197.

Atkins, R. (2015). Depression in Black single mothers: A test of a theoretical model. *Western Journal of Nursing Research, 37*(6), 812-830.

Bresciani Ludvik, M. B. (2015). *Personal interview with Marilee Bresciani, Director of the Integrative Inquiry (INIQ) project at San Diego State University.* December 31, 2015.

ETS. (2013). *Black male teens: Moving to success in the high school years: A statistical profile.* Princeton, NJ: Author.

Flowers, A.M. (2015). The family factor: The establishment of positive academic identity for Black male Engineering majors. *Western Journal of Black Studies. 39*(2).

Flowers, A.M. & Banda, R.M. (2015). The masculinity paradox: Conceptualizing the experiences of men of color in STEM. *The Journal of Culture, Society, and Masculinity 7*(1), 45-60.

Gurian, M., & Stevens, K. (2008). Selections from the minds of boys. In K. Fischer and M. H. Immordino-Yang (Eds.), *The brain and learning* (pp. 405-212). San Francisco, CA: Jossey-Bass.

Harris III, F., & Harper, S. R. (2008). Masculinities go to community college: Understanding male identity socialization and gender role conflict. *New Directions for Community Colleges, 142,* 25-35.

Harris III, F., Palmer, R., & Struve, L.E. (2011). "Cool posing" on campus: A qualitative study of masculinities and gender expression among Black men at private research institution. Journal of Negro Education, 80(1), 47-62.

Howard, T. C. (2014). *Black male(d): Peril and promise in the education of*

African American males. New York, NY: Teachers College Press.

Hudley, C., & Graham, S. (2001). Stereotypes of achievement striving among early adolescents. Social Psychology of Education, 5, 201-224.

Hughes, F. P. (2010). *Children, play, and development.* Thousand Oaks, CA: Sage.

Huynh, V. W. (2014). Ethnic microaggressions and the depressive and somatic symptoms of Latino and Asian American adolescents. Journal of Youth Adolescence, 41, 831-846.

Jackson, J. F. L., & Moore III, J. L. (2008). The African American male crisis in education: A popular media infatuation or needed public policy response? *American Behavioral Scientist, 51*(7), 847-853.

Ladson-Billings, G. (2011). Boyz to men? Teaching to restore Black boys' childhood. *Race Ethnicity and Education, 14*(1), 7-15.

Majors, R. G. (2001). Cool pose: Black masculinity and sports. In S. M. Whitehead, & F. J. Barrett (Eds.), *The masculinities reader* (pp. 209-217). Malden, MA: Blackwell.

Majors, R. G., & Billson, J. M. (1992). *Cool pose: The dilemmas of Black manhood in America.* New York: Lexington Books.

Maslow, A. H. (1943). A theory of human motivation. *Psychological Review, 50,* 370-396.

Mendenhall, R., Bowman, P. J., & Zhang, L. (2013). Single Black mothers' role strain and adaptation across the life course. *Journal of African American Studies, 17,* 74-98.

My Brother's Keeper. (2015). *Economic costs of youth disadvantage and high-return opportunities for change.* Washington, DC: Executive Office of the President of the United States, Council of Economic Advisors.

National Kids Count. (2013a). *Children living in areas of concentrated poverty by race and ethnicity.* Baltimore, MD; Annie E. Casey Foundation.

National Kids Count. (2015b). *Children in Title I schools by race and ethnicity.* Baltimore, MD; Annie E. Casey Foundation.

National Kids Count. (2015c). *Children who live in unsafe communities by race and ethnicity.* Baltimore, MD; Annie E. Casey Foundation.

National Kids Count. (2015d). *Children who have experienced two or more adverse experiences by race and ethnicity.* Baltimore, MD; Annie E. Casey Foundation.

National Kids Count. (2015e). *Children in single-parent families by race.* Baltimore, MD; Annie E. Casey Foundation.

Saenz, V.B., & Ponjuan, L. (2009). The vanishing Latino male in higher education. *Journal of Hispanic Higher Education, 8*(1), 54-89.

Seven Centers Report. *(2014).* Advancing *the* success *of* boys *and* men *of* color: *Recommendations for policy makers.* Contributions from The Center for the Study of Race and Equity in Education, Minority Male Community College Collaborative, Morehouse Research Institute, Project MALES and the Texas Education Consortium for Male Students of Color, Todd Anthony Bell National Resource Center on the African American Male, Black Male Institute, Wisconsin's Equity and Inclusion Laboratory. San Diego, CA: Printing Office.

U.S. Census Bureau. (2013). *Children in extreme poverty (50 percent poverty) by race and ethnicity – 2013 American Community Survey.* Washington, DC: Author.

U.S. Census Bureau. (2014). *Income and poverty in the United States: 2013. Table B-2.* Washington, DC: Author.

Wood, J. L. (2014). Apprehension to engagement in the classroom: Perceptions of Black males in the community college. *International Journal of Qualitative Studies in Education, 27*(6), 785-803.

Wood, J. L., Harris III, F., & White, K. (2015). *Teaching men of color in the community college: A guidebook.* San Diego, CA: Montezuma.

Wood, J. L., & Hilton, A. A. (2013). Moral choices: Towards a conceptual model of Black Male Moral Development (BMMD). *Western Journal of Black Studies, 37*(1), 14-27.

CHAPTER 3

Four Elements of Teaching Excellence

This chapter addresses dispositions that are critical for facilitating successful teaching and learning for boys and young men of color. These concepts include high expectations and authentic care (love). These dispositions are necessary for countering racial-gender stereotypes of Black and Latino males that convey that they are unintelligent and criminals.

Teaching boys and young men of color requires educators to have revised perspectives on them and their abilities. This is a critical component of any effective teaching and learning enterprise for this population. These perspectives require educators to wholly reconsider how they view these males, consciously and unconsciously. Specifically, an understanding of how bias and stereotypes permeate the mind of all individuals, including educators is necessary. Teachers are influenced by common messages about males of color that are evident in wider society. The power of stereotypes about males of color are inescapable. These stereotypes are taught at an early age and reinforced throughout one's life through media and other societal structures. Such messages are engrained in the psyches of all individuals, even within communities of color.

Messages about boys and young men of color convey that they are unintelligent and criminals. To be clear, these messages are present in the minds of all educators.

Commonly, messages about boys and young men of color convey that they are unintelligent and criminals. To be clear, these messages are present in the minds of *all* educators, even those who self-identify as equity-minded and social justice oriented. While the degrees to which these messages are held may differ, all educators, even to a minimal degree, are influenced by these stereotypes. Negative views about boys and young men of color are sometimes proudly and consciously held; however, more often they are maintained unconsciously – through unconscious bias. Unconscious bias encompasses attitudes, beliefs, preferences, and stereotypes about another group that are unconsciously hidden and held (Dovidio, Kawakami, & Gaertner, 2002; Wolverton, Nagaoka & Wolverton, 2015).

Addressing unconscious bias requires concerted action, chief among these actions being recognition and admission of bias (Ross, 2008; Teal, Gill, Green & Crandal, 2012). As noted by Teal et al., (2012) becoming aware of unconscious bias is a developmental process, one that may take time for some educators to feel comfortable acknowledging. Again, the key point here is that all educators have *some* degree of bias that influences their practice. Practices for addressing one's unconscious biases include viewing others (in this case, males of color) as individuals rather than through stereotypical lenses, using self-assessment tools (e.g., Implicit Association Test), and engaging in reflective activities (e.g., journaling). Assuming here that educators reading this volume recognize their hidden biases to some degree, and are actively working to reject them, we offer key perspectives that must replace traditional perspectives of males of color and their success.

All teachers can effectively educate males of color; however, to be successful, they must educate them as males of color.

Educators who do not have a shared cultural background with males of color often question if they can effectively teach and serve them. Often, these comments are made by teachers who have struggled to foster successful outcomes for these males. Yes, we firmly believe that *all* teachers can effectively educate males of color; however, to be successful, they must educate them *as* males of color. What does that mean? It means that these students have unique histories, cultures, identities, and experiences that must be leveraged as assets to improve their educational success. Devoid of this context, educators will struggle to produce equitable outcomes as the learning itself will be segmented and disconnected. In addition to this context, we believe that there are essential elements that must also be in place to effectively educate boys and young men of color (see Figure 1). These elements are foundational for all teachers to be effective in teaching Black and Latino boys and young men.

In the 1960s, a scholar named Nevitt Sanford theorized that two essential elements – challenge and support – were necessary for facilitating the development and success of students. Sanford (1966) argued that all students must be *challenged* with academic learning experiences that are rigorous, pushing them to a higher plane of learning. Within their zone of proximal development, students must be exposed to learning experiences that challenge them to engage new concepts, develop higher order thinking, apply learning in meaningful ways, and understand the connections between seemingly disparate ideas. While the manner in which students are challenged will differ greatly from preschool to high school, challenge is a necessary condition to learning and development. Sanford noted, however, that challenge should also be accompanied with support. Similarly, teachers in the study stated that boys and young men of color, like all students, must be challenged in the classroom. For instance, one Texas teacher stated, "I challenge them to do better than their best. I celebrate their successes with them. I hold them accountable for their behavior and challenge them on their academic efforts."

Sometimes, educators will describe a student as being disengaged or say, "they don't care." Our experience has shown that this is typically a function of not being supported.

Support requires teachers and other educators to provide opportunities to help students grow. Help occurs through teachers being available to meet with students and their families when asked, as well as proactively engaging families when necessary (i.e., in-class, during conferencing, pull-outs, break times, before and after school). Simply put, students must be challenged and have the necessary supports to reach the challenge. Sanford noted that there is an optimal balance between challenge and support. When there is too much challenge and too little support, a student can become discouraged and withdrawn from the learning experience. Sometimes educators will describe a student as being disengaged or say, that "they don't care." Our experience has shown that this is typically a function of not being supported. There are also instances where there is too much support and too little challenge. When this occurs, students experience limited success as they become bored and can feel that school is a waste of their time. Sanford emphasized that both challenge and support be present and balanced for students to experience the most success.

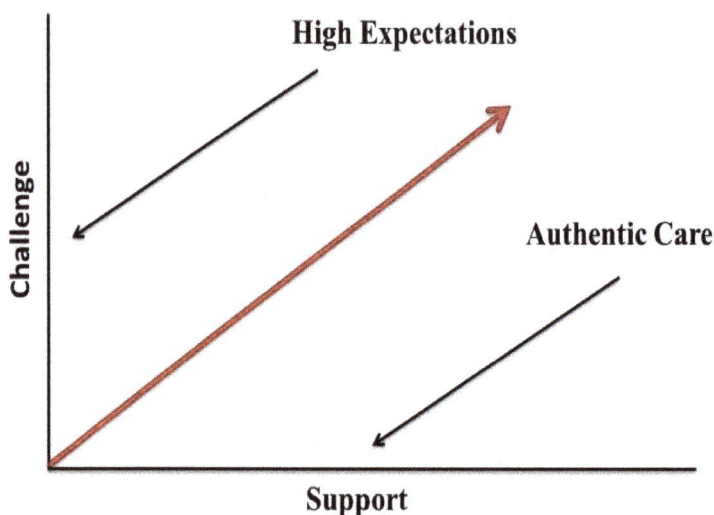

Figure 1: *Four Elements of Excellence for Teaching Males of Color. Used with permission from Wood, Harris III and White (2015).*

While Sanford's model serves as an effective guide for facilitating the success of students in general, it has limited usefulness for Black and Latino males. Like many of the theories that are used to prepare educators, Sanford's theory makes universal assumptions about conditions that are not present in all classrooms for all students. An extensive body of research on the education of children and youth of color has shown that certain preconditions are necessary for challenge and support to take hold. For instance, teachers can challenge males of color with the highest standards possible; yet, if that challenge is not accompanied with *high expectations* regarding the student's ability to meet and exceed those standards, then the challenge will go unmet. More specifically, teachers must believe that a student can 1) reach the challenge set forth; and 2) communicate this belief to students through validating messages about their capacity to do so. Thus, challenge must occur in tandem with high expectations. This can serve to counter the various messages that males of color receive from teachers, peers, and the media that tell them that they are unintelligent and academically inferior. Specifically, one teacher from North Carolina noted that males of color "are not expected to achieve, therefore, expectations seen in the classroom are low." As such, high expectations are a necessary condition for positive acknowledgement of students' abilities.

Teachers must believe that a student can reach the challenge set forth and communicate this belief to students through validating messages about their capacity to do so.

This key point regarding the importance of high expectations was a recurrent theme among teachers with a record of success in educating males of color. The teachers stated that high expectations, rigorous expectations, and standards of accountability must be coupled with encouragement. They stated that teachers must communicate high expectations for students' ability to learn, engage in learning (e.g., turning in homework, completing assignments, studying), excel in school, and demonstrate high standards of behavior. Several teachers noted that the clarity of such messages are key, males of color must know that educators believe in them. For example, one California teacher stated: "I have high expectations and I give a lot of support. It's important for my students to know that *I KNOW* they can achieve and that I will help them get there."

This perspective is reinforced through actions that routinely express high expectations. Specifically, one North Carolina teacher noted the following: "set a level of high expectations from the start, and constantly, and consistently express this to them - what you expect from them academically and socially. The problem sometimes will come when they feel like giving up or quitting, and it is here that you must find ways to inspire and motivate to push through." Thus, motivating students to persist through barriers is a key component of high expectations, as any sign that teachers believe they will not attain a set standard will inhibit success. As noted by a California teacher, "I never lower my standards. I give an abundance of support and make it clear that I believe in their ability to meet my standards, but I never lower my expectations. If I lower my expectations, both academic and behavioral, the students' start to believe that they can't meet the standards."

In addition to challenge and high expectations, teachers can make support available to students, even going so far as to proactively seek out and provide support for students who are on the margins. However, the support will go either unused or be refused if the student doesn't believe that the educator *authentically cares* about them. Authentic care, routinely framed by respondents as *"love"*, is a critical predisposition for males of color to invest their efforts in the educational process. As adeptly noted by a North Carolina teacher "a student doesn't care what you know until they know that you care." Teachers noted that students must know that educators care about them and care for them, suggesting that both disposition and action are necessary for conveying authentic care. Given the external pressures in their lives and stereotypical messages that negate their belonging in school environments, this may be even more important for boys and young men of color than other students

Care about them and care for them... both disposition and action are necessary for conveying authentic care.

Teachers in the study described numerous ways in which authentic care and love are demonstrated to students. Here, we synthesize their comments: educators must communicate to males of color that they are important and that they and their success matter. All communication must convey constant respect and unconditional positive regard for them by allowing students to be themselves without covering up what they are really thinking or feeling. This involves speaking with them and not at them, encouraging them, and letting students know that you are there for them. Verbal actions must be supported through time investment by showing attention to demonstrate their importance and being willing to walk together through challenges. Teachers noted that following through in this manner is critical for building trust. Many educators noted that this necessitates treating them as your own.

Treating students as your own was a salient theme among teachers in the study. For example, one Texas teacher stated that educators must begin "talking to them as you would your son and letting them know you...care for their being and safety." Similarly, a teacher from California noted the following: "I was told early in my teaching career that 'you are the parent, while they are in school,' by parents of color. To me it meant to treat their child as mine. My students know I will go to bat for them. They know I will work hard to help them learn to get the work done. I don't give up. [My] strategy is perseverance. I will go out on the yard at lunch to pull in a child to get the work done and raise the grade." Another way to demonstrate care is to be personally invested in the success of boys and young men of color. This necessitates being committed in a manner where the student knows that their teacher(s) will be disappointed when expectations are not met, while also knowing that this same teacher would show pride and joy when expectations are met.

Regarding the education of Black children, the late Asa Hilliard once said "I have never encountered any children in any group who are not geniuses. There is no mystery on how to teach them. The first thing you do is to treat them like human beings and the second thing you do is love them." Unfortunately, feeling loved and cared about is a missing component in the educational experiences of many males of color. We have heard youth of color exclaim that teachers don't care about them. Younger children often struggle to articulate this perception, usually communicating this view by saying "My teacher doesn't like me."

Generally, the message conveyed by educators is not the message received by students. Many teachers may in fact love and care about the children and youth that they work with; however, they may also struggle to demonstrate this to their students. We find that unconscious bias and racial-gender microaggressions (common, subtle racial slights) serve to unknowingly send mixed messages to students. In essence, a child can be told that they are cared about, but unconscious body language may suggest an alternative perspective. Research from communication in education has shown that when there is a conflict between the verbal and non-verbal, students will believe the non-verbal. Therefore, educators may believe that they are communicating care to students when in fact they are not.

A child can be told that they are cared about, but unconscious body language may suggest an alternative perspective... when there is a conflict between the verbal and non-verbal, students will believe the non-verbal.

In concluding this chapter, we present a quote from a California teacher that encompasses concepts embodied within this chapter: "Love, love, love our children. Love them enough to challenge them and not expect them to conform to giving less than they are fully capable of. Love them to reward them for their accomplishments - no matter how small. Love them to ask what THEY feel is needed for them to accomplish their dreams (be humble and don't assume you know). Love them to call home and do home visits to express your respect for their origins and show interest in their lives. Love them to understand that our structural racist system is broken, having caused a social reality that negatively impacts families of color. Love them to know you are not the savior of their reality because assuming so is a blatant disrespect to their potential and self-worth. Love them to fight for their education - and tell them, so in order for them to find an ally they can trust. Love them because you may be the only one that ever shows or tells them so."

REFERENCES

Dovidio, J. F., Kawakami, K., & Gaertner, S. L. (2002). Implicit and explicit prejudice and interracial interaction. *Journal of Personality and Social Psychology, 82*(1), 62–68.

Ross, H. (2008). Proven strategies for addressing unconscious bias in the workplace. *CDO Insights, 2*(5), 1-18.

Sanford, N. (1966). *Self and society*. New York, NY: Atherton.

Teal, C. R., Gill, A. C., Green, A. R., & Crandall, S. (2012). Helping medical learners recognize and manage unconscious bias toward certain patient groups. *Medical Education, 46,* 80-88.

Wolverton, A., Nagaoka, L., & Wolverton, M. (2015). *Women's accounts of how choice shape STEM careers*. Sterling, VA: Stylus.

Wood, J. L., Harris III, F., & White, K. (2015). *Teaching men of color in the community college: A guidebook*. San Diego, CA: Montezuma.

CHAPTER 4

Relationship Building Strategies

This chapter discusses relationship building strategies that are essential for building rapport and trust with males of color and their families. The chapter highlights the importance of relationships as a critical foundation for teaching and learning that precedes effective pedagogical practice.

As foregrounded in the previous chapter, relationships are a critical cornerstone for enhancing the learning experience of boys and young men of color. Teachers and other educational professionals have a responsibility to build relationships with males of color and their families. There are a number of critical benefits for teachers who build rapport and trust with Black and Latino males through their relationships with them. These relationships enable educators to: a) support students' continued development by understanding academic and personal strengths and recognizing areas of necessary growth; b) better recognize and account for barriers that males of color face in their external lives; c) leverage unique assets that males of color bring to learning environments; d) build a foundation of trust, mutual respect, rapport, and authentic care; e) facilitate the growth of self-esteem, confidence, and ownership in the learning experience; and f) break down racial-gender stereotypes and unhealthy notions of masculinity that inhibit success in school.

Positive relationships with males of color are the critical foundation to any effective teaching and learning enterprise for this population.

The benefits of building positive relationships with students and their families cannot be understated. According to Wood, Harris III and White (2015), positive relationships with males of color are *the* critical foundation to any effective teaching and learning enterprise for this population. Stated differently, it does not matter how well you teach, if you do not have a relationship with these males, then your efforts will be in vain. More specifically, educators can develop cogent lesson plans, employ rigorous standards, and be very engaging presenters, yet the manifold benefits of these efforts will be marred when a positive relationship is lacking.

To highlight this point, Wood et al., developed the Pyramid of Student Success (see Figure 2). At the base of the pyramid, is a relational dynamic that is typified by trust, mutual respect, and authentic care. Upon this foundation rests practices employed by educators (e.g., teachers, counselors, classroom aids) that are effective and engaging. At the top of the pyramid is student success, broadly defined, encompassing student achievement, learning, and development. Student success is achieved when both the relational foundation and effective and engaging practices are in place. The absence of either segment of the pyramid inhibits student success. They argue that "enhanced relationships (coupled with effective and engaging pedagogy) play an important role in mediating the effects of external pressures, racial-gender stereotypes, male gender role socialization, and academic preparation issues that contaminate the experiences and comprise success" (p. 30) for males of color.

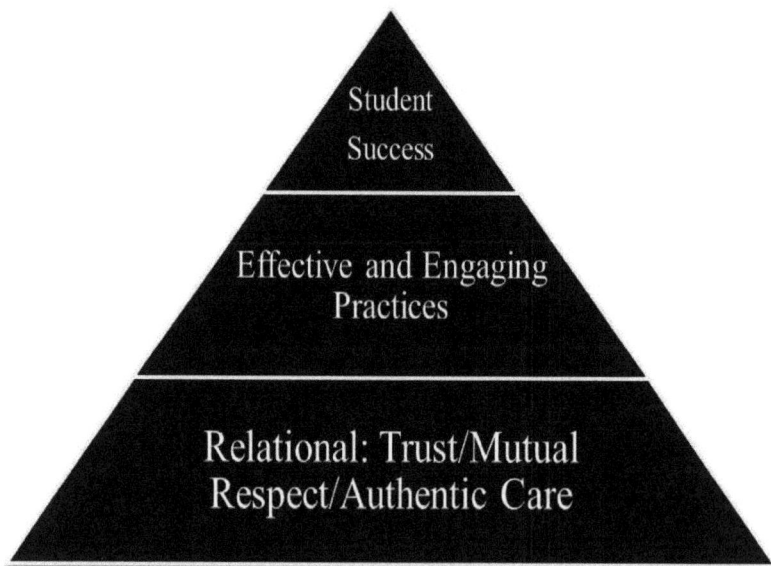

Figure 2: *Pyramid of Student Success for Boys and Young Men of Color. Used with permission from Wood, Harris III and White (2015).*

In addition to the principles of trust, mutual respect, and authentic care, teachers from the study argued that patience is also a necessary condition for establishing positive relationships. In acknowledging the time needed to account for and address the myriad of barriers facing boys and young men of color (e.g., external life pressures, racial-gender stereotypes), they noted that educators must also recognize that relationships (as with learning and development) take time to develop. For this population, the necessary foundation of relationships as a precursor to student learning and development means that a high level of patience is critical. Several teachers noted that a little more patience may be necessary for this population, but the pay-off for this patience can also be greater for males of color than other students.

RELATIONSHIP-BUILDING STRATEGIES

Guided by these principles, the teachers in this study offered numerous strategies that can be used by educators to build relationships with students and their families. We begin with strategies focused on parents, guardians, and families of boys and young men of color.

RELATIONSHIP BUILDING WITH FAMILIES

Families should play a critical role in the educational experiences of Black and Latino males. While the nature of the family structure will vary greatly between children and youth, the strategies offered by teachers in this study demonstrate that need for intensive, on-going opportunities to engage in their child's learning. For simplicity, we refer to all stakeholders (e.g., parents, guardians, family, extended family) as *family*. Having a relationship with a student's family is essential for fostering genuine conversations with families about the progress, needs, and interests of their child.

Recognize that Families Want the Best

Prior to establishing any relationship with family members, educators must internally consider perspectives they have about students' families. As noted earlier in this volume, it is common for educators to harbor deficit perspectives that blame students, their families, and their communities for academic challenges. More specifically, some educators make judgments about family members and students, believing that the students don't care and neither do their families. These perspectives can be held consciously or unconsciously, but can greatly influence when and how educators interact with family members.

As found by Harper and Associates (2014) in a study involving 500 individual interviews with Black and Latino high school males, families regularly convey the importance of an education. These messages begin at an early age. Even in cases where family members themselves had not fulfilled their educational goals, they emphasized the importance of school. Expressing this point, Harper and Associates (2014) stated that:

> "participants did not mistake their parents' educational pathways as disregard for the value of formal schooling. It was instead the opposite – they knew parents wanted them and their siblings to be better educated, struggle less, and have higher-status jobs that offer respectability and financial security. (p. 15)

Similarly, teachers in this study noted that the vast majority of family members care greatly for their sons' success in school. As recommended by a California teacher "CONNECT with the family. All families want what is best for their children so become a team member." Similarly, a Texas teacher stated "Keeping the family involved. Most African American parents want the best for their children." Like all families, some parents have greater exposure to ways that they can best support their sons' education while others may need some guidance. For Latino males, it should be acknowledged that some Latino cultures pedestal teachers in a manner where questioning and advocacy on the part of the family may be perceived as disrespectful to the teacher. Thus, it is important to avoid assuming that an apprehension from parents equates to lack of care. Consciously acknowledging that families want the best for their sons is key to ensuring that interactions with them produce positive relationships that can benefit their child's education.

Consciously acknowledging that families want the best for their sons is key.

Establish Connections with the Family

The educators in this study overwhelmingly recommended that teachers establish relationships with students' families. They noted that doing so could aid the educational process through home support of what is being taught in the classroom. For example, a California teacher said, "Get parents involved. With parents involved, you have a generational connection to the family. The parents can help drive points of emphasis to the student while they are not in school or show them another relevant example of the lesson you taught in class." Teachers noted that a part of building trust with a family is showing an authentic interest in the child or youth. A desire to learn about students' likes and dislikes is key to building a relationship with the student and leveraging personal interests to make the curriculum culturally relevant. Family members possess the deepest insight into the interests of males of color. As such, teachers should use initial and ongoing opportunities to ask family members to provide them with information about the child that they can use to support their learning and development.

Maintain Constant Contact

Maintaining and advancing relationships with family members requires constant contact as well as intrusivity. Teachers in the study mentioned the importance of emailing and phoning parents to proactively update them on what is taking place with the child. For example, one California teacher stated, "Take the time to call home and discuss the habits or behaviors that are not expected in your class. More often than not, parents will be your biggest advocate. Even with high school students/seniors you may be surprised at the results you will get from a phone call about inappropriate behavior or falling grades." Of course, communication with family should also occur around positive performance as well. The key here is maintaining constant contact with family members so when issues arise at home or at school communication can take place. Some teachers talked about the importance of gaining permission from families to be in constant contact, allowing them to have ownership in what may be a greater level of communication than they have previously experienced interacting with teachers. One North Carolina teacher discussed approaching this conversation through the lens of coaching, saying "I challenge mothers to let me "coach" their sons in the classroom. If the athletic coach can push on the athletic field or court so can I!" Gaining permission to "coach" created an opportunity for greater access and also served to frame a universal understanding that the relationship with the student would be more intensive and direct.

Maintain constant contact with family members, so when issues arise at home or at school, communication can take place.

With Family Permission, Be Intrusive into Home Context

Teachers noted that, in some cases, it was important to go beyond phone calls and emails with students' families. With family permission, some teachers even discussed the importance of conducting home visits. They noted that doing so enabled them to have a better understanding of the family and establish greater rapport with family members. For example, one California teacher stated "connecting to the families is BIG! Don't be afraid to call home or stop by their home. Seeing their teacher in their turf makes them vulnerable. You often see their hidden truth - whether good or bad - and they know they can't put up a front of tough guy before you. Knowing their momma's …gives an educator a better perspective on HOW to reach them." While not specific to the home context, some teachers also discussed attending after school events (e.g., sports, theatrical, and music activities) that take place at school with the specific goal of supporting students' external lives. This is an important strategy for building rapport with students and their families, especially if when informed in advance that they will be attending the events with a specific interest in supporting their son.

Demonstrate High Expectations

When engaging with family members, educators must convey positive messages about their students that demonstrate their high expectations for them. Low expectations will be perceived as uncaring, and will serve as a natural barrier to building relationships of trust, mutual respect, and authentic care. Remember here, for this population, all messages will be filtered through family members own encounters with racial-gender stereotypes as well as their own experiences in school. Thus, conveying high expectations for student performance is critical. This strategy becomes even more important when the communication with the parent(s) includes feedback that addresses behavioral or performance corrections. In such instances, positive messaging must be embedded within the communication with the parent. As such, instead of saying "Alex is standing up during circle time" or "Terrence is not paying attention in class" a teacher can say "Alex is a great listener, we just need to work on staying seated during circle time, but tomorrow is another opportunity" or "Terrence has so much to offer to the class discussions, we had some rough spots today with his attention, but when he is fully focused his contributions are powerful, so we need to still work on that."

Altogether, the aforementioned strategies highlight the importance of building trust, being intrusive, and having an anti-deficit perspective. These are key principles that cut across grade levels that can be used by teachers to better facilitate the success of boys and young men of color through relationships with their families. While this section talked about relational strategies with family members, the next section will address approaches for establishing similar relationships with Black and Latino males.

RELATIONSHIP BUILDING WITH MALES OF COLOR

Building positive relationships with boys and young men of color is essential for breaking down societal stereotypes about them and their abilities.

As noted, building positive relationships with boys and young men of color is essential for breaking down societal stereotypes about them and their abilities. In framing the recommendations for relationship-building, teachers commented on the importance of understanding why these strategies are so critical to student success. In particular, teachers noted that these boys are either ignored or vilified. For example, one Florida teacher stated, "I try to specifically target the young men of color at the beginning of school year and develop a positive relationship. They are so used to being ignored or devalued by society." Moreover, a teacher from New York noted asserted, "boys and young men of color are unseen as individuals. They are accustomed to being seen as "one of them," society's most vilified group. It seems they become so used to being seen as representative of that group, they assume people do not see them for who they are, as unique individuals, and this causes them to face the world with resentment and defensiveness. So, I make a deliberate effort to communicate (verbally and non-) that I see them as a single entity." Grounded by these perspectives, the teachers offered a number of relationship building strategies for working with Black and Latino males in education.

Refer to Them by Name

The first and most important relationship-building strategy that should be used with boys and young men of color is to know their name. It is critical that teachers know students' full names; refer to them by their last name or name they prefer to be called by; know how to pronounce their name; as well as use their name when referring to and interacting with them. Knowing a student's name can be a powerful way of conveying that their presence and personhood is important to educators. This is essential, because names often serve to shape students' identities. For example, one California teacher stated: "One strategy used is to greet the males by positive identification such as: Gentleman, Young Man/Men, Mister, and their full name. This is to give identity to who they are and who they are becoming. Knowing the name they actually go by. Know how to say it." A number of teachers also emphasized the importance of referring to students by their last name as a sign of respect. For example, two teachers from North Carolina stated "Address the student by their last name. For example: Good Morning Mr. Gill, I'm glad to see you. For most of our Black males, they will never be addressed by mister unless it is in a court of law. Teachers must build respect" and "I generally called male students by their last name. By doing this, I am showing them the same respect that I require and expect."

Knowing a student's name can be powerful way of conveying that their presence and personhood is important to educators.

As noted, educators must also know how to correctly pronounce students names. Pronouncing their names incorrectly can be invalidating and communicate a lack of importance. If a teacher is unsure how to say an individual's name correctly, the best policy is to ask them or their families. This may be humbling for the educator, but is far less challenging than the academic challenges teachers set before their students. As explained by Harvell (2016), "educators constantly challenge students to learn information that they may struggle with. Teachers speak with an argot of academic lingo specific to their discipline, communicate new concepts and theories, and constantly require students to push themselves in their learning and development. Any educator who downplays the importance of saying a student's name correctly does so from a standpoint of privilege that their students rarely have". Finally, saying a student's name correctly and/or referring to them by the name they go by is critical to avoiding disciplinary issues. We have witnessed boys of color in preschool and kindergarten being referred to by names they don't recognize (e.g., improperly pronounced, using a first name when a child goes by their middle name) and have been reprimanded or criticized for not responding to teacher requests.

Learn About Them with Interest

Beyond knowing their names, teachers in this study noted the importance of learning about Black and Latino males. They suggested that learning about them requires asking questions and being authentically interested in what they have to say. For instance, one Florida teacher stated, "ask questions- many people are nervous or scared to ask kids questions especially kids that are different from them or culturally different, in order to understand kids I need to know about them, I ask and I am interested." Similarly, a teacher from Georgia noted, "One strategy I use is to get to know the student outside of what they do in the classroom. I talk to them about their interests and experiences. I do this so that the student will know that I have a genuine interest in their success inside and outside of the classroom." Some teachers even used the word "delight" to describe the expression of interest that is necessary for helping students to open up. This type of interest is necessary for conveying care and building trust. The teachers discussed a wide array of areas that teachers' learning about a student should occur, including prior learning experiences, students' families, home culture, language, external barriers, personal interests, thoughts and opinions, likes and dislikes, and aspirations among numerous other factors. Of these areas, culture was emphasized the most among educators. For instance, a Georgia teacher urged other educators to "Understand the culture. It is very important to understand the culture of the child. Some ways of communicating might be seen as disrespectful however they are just an example of the culture and what is acceptable within."

Some teachers even used the word "delight" to describe the expression of interest that is necessary for helping students to open up. This type of interest is necessary for conveying care and building trust.

Finally, a few teachers noted the role that structured activities play in helping to gain initial information, for instance, one California teacher stated that they employ a "survey on day one to discuss what's new with students so that I am always learning about students as each group has its own cultural architecture." That being said, such surveys should serve as starter strategy, as the majority of teachers noted that the one-on-one dynamic is the most meaningful and impactful avenue for learning about students.

Finally, in addition to learning about students personally, it is also critical that educators learn about them academically. In particular, asking questions about their prior experiences with educators, subjects they like, and perceptions of school (in tandem with personal information) is essential for creating instructional plans and goals for each student.

Be Fully Present During Conversations

As just mentioned, boys and young men of color often experience being ignored or unwanted in educational settings. Thus, establishing relationships with this population requires interactions where the educator is fully present. This can be difficult for educators who rely on multi-tasking to accomplish the numerous duties and responsibilities that they have in a condensed time frame. However, doing so is critical to the success of these males. Building personal relationships takes time, and for a population of students who often feel invisible and unimportant, time investment can serve as a true indicator of authentic care. As noted by a teacher from Florida, "Always make time for young men of color no matter how much is going on in your life." Teachers in the study noted that when educators are fully present, students are much more likely to reciprocate the attention. Being present requires that teachers be fully focused on students (with appropriate body language and eye contact), listen to them, and validate their emotions. As extolled by a California teacher, "Listen, listen, listen. The students will speak their truth but when you try to dictate and tell them what they need instead of listening to what their telling you they need, they will keep everything inside." One New York teacher further commented, "I make eye contact. I ask them questions and interact with them casually and personally, sometimes more than with my other students."

Regular Check-Ins

Learning about students is not a static process…Checking in with Black and Latino males is a proactive strategy that can be used to support, monitor, and reach out to students.

Learning about students is not a static process; teachers repeatedly noted the importance of regularly checking in with students. Checking in with Black and Latino males is a proactive strategy that can be used to support, monitor, and reach out to students when needed. Proactively checking in communicates a sense of care and concern for the student. Checking in can be facilitated in several ways. One strategy includes have set questions at the beginning of a class as part of a prompt that enables teachers to collect and streamline information gathering from students. As suggested by one California teacher, use a "Check in question. At least three times a week I take attendance by asking check in questions. The questions range from 'how are you feeling today?' to 'what's your favorite sport?' to 'what time did you go to bed last night?' This helps me get to know my students outside of their academic identity."

Regularly checking in also leverages the one-on-one dynamic of asking questions and demonstrating interest that is critical for learning about students. Educators emphasized that learning about students is an ongoing process, as the relationship builds, the questions typically evolve and become more specific. For example, if a student has confided in a teacher that they are experiencing a certain challenge at home, the teacher can then ask specific follow-up questions to the student during subsequent conversations. While checking in should occur regularly, it becomes even more important when there are changes in students' dispositions, levels of engagement, or physical demeanor. Teachers should be cognizant of such changes to ensure that they demonstrate care when issues arise.

Appropriate Disclosing

Disclosing was a common strategy discussed by exemplar teachers in this study. Disclosing involves revealing personal information about oneself to build rapport with another. In this case, it involves teachers appropriately revealing personal information that allows them to build greater levels of trust, mutual respect, and authentic care with boys and young men of color. Teachers repeatedly noted the benefits of sharing personal life struggles and success, as a mechanism for breaking down walls and discussing the benefit of being focused and driven towards one's dreams. They noted that this approach helped to humanize them, allowing students to see them as more relatable. Some teachers noted that being vulnerable in front of them, allowed for students to feel more comfortable opening up with them. This was seen as a critical pathway for fostering authentic conversations as well as trust. Teachers also noted that disclosing can be a motivational tool, as students can see someone who has experienced struggles and overcome those struggles in achieving success. One important caveat with this approach is not to make statements about equivalency (e.g., "my struggle is like yours, I have struggled too") or in any way dismiss the unique challenges faced by males of color. Instead, the goal is to be more relatable and provide motivation by discussing challenges faced and personal life information.

Teachers noted that being vulnerable in front of them, allowed for students to feel more comfortable being vulnerable with them as well. This was seen as a critical pathway for fostering authentic conversations as well as trust.

Be "Real" and "Down to Earth'

To foster authentic dialogue that builds positive relationships and creates trust, teachers must be 'down to earth.' Being 'down to earth' necessitates that teachers have 'real' conversations about 'real' experiences and issues that they face. In tandem, these concepts suggest relatability and authenticity. This is a key concept for boys and young men of color who are often untrusting of teachers, beginning at early levels of schooling and growing as they traverse the academic pipeline. Teachers in this study gave a number of examples of what it means to be 'down to earth', they include being willing to laugh at yourself and with them when appropriate, conveying respect, being supportive, and creating a sense of safety to have challenging conversations about academic and personal matters. Moreover, many teachers talked about the importance of "talking *with* students and not *at* them." For instance, one North Carolina teacher stated, "building a relationship that is positive would be my first strategy, letting them feel a sense that you care and you understand that maybe things have not been easy, but together we are going to begin to make them better. This will also take building a level of understanding and sometimes will mean bringing yourself to their level, so that you can talk with them and not talk over them."

Further, teachers noted that being "real" means to be honest and truthful. One teacher from Florida said, "Don't sugar-coat life," you have to have strong enough relationships where you can tell them what you really think. Multiple teachers noted that this entailed a willingness to tell them what they are up against (e.g., what it means to be a Black or Latino man in today's society). In addition, teachers noted that being "real" encompassed a willingness to talk about any school appropriate subject matter. As noted by a New York teacher, if you aren't willing to talk, this can lead to shame and "shame leads to unprocessed emotions and a very skewed view of the world. I'd rather get it out there, say it aloud and process it with them, rather than remain silent." Being "down to earth" and "real" does not suggest that the necessary barrier between teacher and student be nullified. As noted earlier, this strategy is about fostering relatability and authenticity.

Motivational Messaging

It is absolutely critical that teachers and other educators engage in positive, motivational messaging that counters stereotypes and actual barriers that the students may face.

As evidenced in earlier chapters, there are many challenges facing males of color in education, the workforce, and the criminal justice system. It would be easy for boys of color to perceive success, both in school and later in life, to be unattainable and unrealistic. The statistics of success in these areas are reinforced through racial-gender stereotypes that are ubiquitously perpetuated in all social venues. As a result, it is absolutely critical that teachers and other educators engage in positive, motivational messaging that counter stereotypes and actual barriers that the students may face. These messages are crucial for revising negative self-fulfilling perspectives that boys may have about their futures. For example, teachers repeatedly noted the importance of messaging that conveys a positive picture of future opportunities. In discussing the importance of such messaging, one New York teacher commented on the stark reality that many students face, saying, "We talk about what life and study skills we need to succeed. It's not enough just to throw numbers and books at kids and expect them to succeed in a world that expects them to fail or at best only reach a certain place. I will sum this up in an example, a young man in my class once said to me, 'It doesn't matter what I learn. When I grow up I will go to jail just like my brothers.' We worked all year long on changing that mantra. He needed to believe that there is more." Regardless of background, it should be expected that many Black and Latino males will face perceptional challenges about success in school and life. As offered by the exemplar teachers, here are some motivational messages provided by exemplar teachers that are necessary for creating successful schooling conditions.

- Work ethic – Messages about work ethic that note the importance of hard work, determination, persistence, and perseverance (e.g., "keep pushing," "hard work pays off"). *Note: This should be done while acknowledging that they will face barriers that others will not, as to avoid negating the unique realities of boys and young men of color.*

- Validation – Communicating high expectations about students' abilities and aptitudes (e.g., "you can do it," "you can succeed," "I believe in you," "you're so smart," "you are so great!," "you deserve the best," "you are a person of great value," "Yo soy Joaquín," and "great job." *Note: While these generic examples of validation can work well, validation is even more powerful when tied to specific activities or tasks (e.g., "you did really well on..." or "great job on....")*

- Resilience – Recognizing barriers and telling students that they have the ability to succeed in the face of these barriers (e.g., "it's not how you fall down, but how you pick yourself up," "education is the most powerful weapon you possess," "we live in a prejudicial world, but that is not a reason to fail").

- Control – Telling them that they have control over their academic futures and life (e.g., "knowledge is power," "failing is not an option," "what is in your control? Your education!")

- Positive futures – Messages that encourage them to consider a positive, intrinsically worthwhile future (e.g., "you will go to college someday," "you can create the life you want for yourself," "envision yourself in the future," "education gives you the power to change your destination").

A key determinant of the effectiveness of positive messaging is the degree that the student perceives the message as genuine. Boys and young men of color can be very wary of educators who affirm them, usually this is a function of prior exposure to these messages. However, motivational messages may be so foreign to them, that they may be initially weary of why they are receiving them. So, expect push-back. Intensive, authentic, pervasive messaging is needed over time to counter years of stereotypes directed towards boys and young men of color. These positive messages will demonstrate care and foster relationships of trust for these males.

This chapter has addressed a number of strategies that are necessary for building relationships with boys and young men of color as well as their families. These strategies must be used routinely as teachers build, maintain, and extend positive personal relationships with students and their families. Guided by this foundation, the next chapter will address effective and engaging pedagogical practices that are necessary for educating males of color in education.

REFERENCES

Harvell, K. (2016). *Personal communication with Kalvin Harvell, faculty member at Henry Ford College.* January 7, 2016.

Harper, S. R., & Associates. (2014). *Succeeding in the city: A report from the New York City Black and Latino male high school achievement study.* Philadelphia, PA: University of Pennsylvania, Center for the Study of Race and Equity in Education.

Wood, J. L., Harris III, F., & White, K. (2015). *Teaching men of color in the community college: A guidebook.* San Diego, CA: Montezuma.

CHAPTER 5

Teaching and Learning Strategies

This chapter will address pedagogical strategies that emerged from the exemplar teachers study. Specifically, this chapter will begin with a focus on incorporating culturally relevant pedagogy into the classroom. Then, additional strategies for enhancing the education of boys and young men of color will be explicated.

One of the most salient themes discussed by exemplar teachers focused on the use of culturally relevant pedagogy. Teachers noted that it is critical for classroom content and teaching delivery to be relevant to the historical legacies and contemporary lives and experiences of boys and young men of color. A key priority for educators is ensuring that students are able to apply what they are learning to the real world and to use this learning to improve their lives. Prior to engaging a curriculum and delivery style that is culturally relevant, exemplar teachers noted that educators must train themselves to see students' culture through an anti-deficit lens. They noted that an asset-based lens was critical to teachers prioritizing the use of culturally relevant pedagogy. Teachers also highlighted the importance of recognizing how different cultures and peoples are privileged in educational settings, course content, and delivery style.

A key priority for educators is ensuring that students are able to apply what they are learning to the real world and to use this learning to improve their lives.

As noted by Ladson-Billings (1992), culturally relevant pedagogy "empowers students intellectually, socially, emotionally, and politically by using cultural referents to impart knowledge, skills, and attitudes" (p. 382). More specifically, exemplar teachers noted that culturally relevant pedagogy is critical to student success for boys and young men of color. Culturally relevant pedagogy communicates to students that educators value their perspectives and beliefs, makes course material more meaningful and easier to understand, increases student engagement, connects students to class learning, and creates a greater sense of belonging in school. It is critical that cultural relevance be deeply rooted in all learning strategies and activities. Otherwise, the benefit of strategies advocated by exemplar teachers will not be maximized.

TEACHING AND LEARNING STRATEGIES

What follows are some key teaching and learning strategies discussed by teachers with a proven record of success in educating boys and young men of color. We begin by returning to our discussion of culturally relevant practices.

Culturally Relevant Content

Cultural relevance is not as simple as replacing the name "John" with "Juan" in a word problem, rather, it is a pervasive integration of ideas, images, texts, and experiences that reflect the culture and lives of students.

The vast majority of exemplar teachings discussed the importance of making sure that the curriculum is relevant to the lives socio-cultural experiences of students. Cultural relevance is not as simple as replacing the name "John" with "Juan" in a word problem, rather, it is a pervasive integration of ideas, images, texts, and experiences that reflect the culture and lives of students. As noted by one California teacher: "[I] try and create an equitable classroom by being conscious of the curriculum I use and to try and incorporate diverse narratives whenever possible, this includes explicit critical discussions during learning and *all* general class functions. For students of color, this is especially important, because of a need for all students to see and feel affirmation surrounding culture and experiences…connecting to the student both culturally and experientially is also crucial so they can build new knowledge from their previous experience and knowledge."

Another teacher in California noted that implementing culturally relevant teaching requires a curriculum that "brings in activities that have relevance in historical context, current events, and importance to the group." As a result, educators must incorporate both contemporary and historical information in pursuing relevancy. Exposing students to historical figures and events helps them to understand how people from their same heritage have contributed to knowledge development and overcame similar barriers for life success. Given the pervasive exclusion of such figures and events from the current curriculum, teachers may need to be intentional about helping students to make initial connections as to *why* the material is relevant to them. As recommended by a Texas teacher, educators must "introduce them to historical role models of individuals who overcame similar circumstances and became successful."

Educators should be cautious about focusing on slavery, the civil rights movement, and labor rights movements as the mechanism for translating content in relevant ways.

When incorporating culturally relevant teaching, it is critical that educators avoid stereotyping communities of color. From a historical perspective, educators should be cautious about focusing on topics such as slavery, the civil rights movement, and labor rights movements as *the* mechanism for translating content in relevant ways. These events are rooted in historical subjugation and merely serve to reinforce stereotypical notions about people of color (Wood, Harris III & White, 2015). This is not to say that these events should be excluded altogether; rather, educators should focus on bringing in other historical events that can lend support to classroom learning. As noted by a California teacher, "find the greatest parts to celebrate and allow [students] to make and see the connections to their own lives. They need to understand that struggle leads to success."

Contemporary examples should prioritize focusing on current figures such as business leaders, politicians, activists, scientists, and researchers who are in fields where males of color are lacking. This can serve to open the minds of boys and young men to alternative opportunities for their futures that they may not have previously considered. That being said, examples from athletics and entertainment can be used; however, this must be carefully approached to avoid further socializing Black and Latino boys to see these fields as their only options.

Educators at all levels of the pipeline (e.g., K-12, post-secondary education) and specialists across disciplines (e.g., math, science, social studies) highlighted the benefits of culturally relevant teaching. Notwithstanding, the greatest emphasis was placed on the benefits of this approach for teaching English. Exemplar teachers noted that reading materials used in their classes should include: a focus on people of color; works written by authors of color; books with diverse characters; and stories that connect to themes relevant in students' personal lives. One California teacher provided a beautiful illustration of how to incorporate culturally relevant pedagogy. This teacher stated that educators should, "integrate the practical application to the theory behind the teaching. Giving students a real-life connection, it helps them see the BIG picture and relevance to education. For example, when teaching poetry, I start off by displaying Tupac Shakur's *The Rose that Grew From Concrete*. Oddly, although the students have heard Tupac's songs, most do not realize he is the author. Once they know that rap/hip-hop/banda/ranchero music can be analyzed for literal meaning, they are hooked and begin to bring and share their favorite songs to contribute to the class. Getting their interest in something they connect to, allows me to remove the filters that resist learning from occurring. Another example of reaching out to their experience is using the soccer commentator, Enrique Bermudes to engage my Latino men in understanding descriptive writing and analogies (the commentator is well known for 'painting the picture' for the fans when he narrates a soccer encounter). After discussing how Bermudes is a famous commentator, mainly thanks to his talented writing, the boys begin to pay more attention to their word choice and descriptive writing."

Culturally relevant teaching is more time intensive, because the traditional curriculum and resources lack examples that relate to boys of color. As such, educators must be more intentional, aware, and innovative.

While there are numerous benefits for employing culturally relevant content, engaging this strategy is not without challenge. According to one California teacher, "Too often, in classrooms and narratives of learning, students of color are not afforded the privilege of cultural connection to that which they are learning from the traditional curriculum." Similarly, a Texas teacher stated, "[I] try to use books and stories that my students can identify with. [However, there are] very limited examples of stories where young men of color are the main and strong character." As a result, several teachers noted that culturally relevant teaching is more time intensive, because the traditional curriculum and resources lack examples that relate to boys of color requiring educators to be more intentional, aware, and innovative. As noted by a teacher from California "young men of color need to see themselves in the work. Without generations of success within their schema, teachers must innovate."

Address Racism and Stereotypes

Exemplar teachers extolled the importance of recognizing that racism exists and trying to understand how young men experience racism and perceive race. Moreover, they discussed the importance of implementing a curriculum that explicitly addresses race and social justice issues. In this vein, one California teacher said, "we look at the hard to look at, discussions of genocide and racism. I chose edgy books that will engage all my students." Implementing a curriculum of this nature requires being proactive in addressing race and embracing racial discussions that emerge naturally. As adeptly stated by a New York teacher, "I am unafraid when the topic arises naturally and also find ways to bring it into the classroom discussions. So much of the current racial tensions in the nation are because we are frightened to talk about race; we keep ourselves in the dark about it. But things grow in the dark. I allow my classroom to be a place where we shine light on race and it's a safe place to talk about it. I make it clear I am willing to and interested in learning from my students about their experience of and ideas about this issue." Several teachers discussed the benefits of engaging an openly anti-racist curriculum, noting that it leads to a greater sense of resiliency among young men of color and enhanced comradery among all students in the classroom.

Addressing racism also requires that teachers actively counter pervasive stereotypes about boys and young men of color.

Addressing racism also requires that teachers actively counter pervasive stereotypes about boys and young men of color. Socialization is powerful, the messages that boys of color receive about what it means to be male and to be Black or Latino inform their identity development. The challenge is that many of the messages that they receive about these identities are guided by racism and informed by stereotypes. As discussed in Chapter 2, males of color are stereotypically viewed as unintelligent and criminals. Addressing these issues means to talk about stereotypes in class and to work with boys of color in exploring and/or recognizing how they may have bought into these views. For example, it is not uncommon for boys of color to embrace the notion that intelligence and being smart is reserved for girls. As noted by a Texas teacher, "I instill in [boys of color] that they can be popular and smart and still gain acceptance by their peers by not compromising on principles. It is important that these young men know that they have to be true to themselves."

Employ Mastery Learning Principles

Mastery learning was articulated by exemplar teachers as being critical to academic success for boys and young men of color. As noted by Jacobsen, Eggen, and Kauchak (2002), mastery learning "is an instructional strategy that allows students to progress at their own pace through a unit of study that has preset, established goals" (p. 236). They explicate seven primary steps for mastery-learning, including: 1) identifying the learning objectives; 2) employing an introductory quiz to determine students prerequisite skills; 3) instruction on the topic of interest (often in groups); 4) formative evaluation of learning to determine areas of needed growth; 5) corrective action via alternative instruction; 6) enhanced learning opportunities for students who demonstrate mastery (while further corrective actions are deployed for those needing further intervention); and 7) a cumulative evaluation of learning.

While these represent the technical steps of mastery learning, exemplar teachers focused most intently on the concept of ensuring that students have actually mastered the course material at hand before moving forward to additional material. This approach is in stark contrast to traditional teaching approaches where students are taught information at one point in time. The traditional approach serves to compound learning gaps over time, as concepts are often scaffolded. In contrast, a California teacher noted that "mastery grading on proficiency scales helps students understand their strengths, weaknesses and areas for growth, motivating them to re-assess and master concepts rather than accept what is "handed to them" for a grade."

The teachers in this study noted that mastery learning is an important strategy for supporting all students, but has an intensified benefit for boys of color. For example, boys are socialized to be strong and avoid seeking help. Moreover, boys of color are even more reluctant to seek help for fear of actualizing stereotypes about their intelligence. As a result, teachers in the study noted that mastery principles assume that some students will need to be taught information multiple times and in multiple ways. According to a Texas teacher, this is important as boys of color will have a heightened focus of "saving face" in front of peers. As a result, mastery approaches structure the learning environment in a manner where gaps cannot be glossed over; instead, there are checks for comprehension, and re-teaching material and test retakes are embedded to create an environment of intrusive support.

Boys are socialized to be strong and avoid seeking help. Moreover, boys of color are even more reluctant to seek help for fear of actualizing stereotypes about their intelligence.

Foster Critical Reflection

Critical reflection was another recurrent theme expressed by teachers in the exemplar study. According to Howard (2003), "critical reflection is the type of processing that is critical to the concept of culturally relevant pedagogy...[as] reflective action can be a more useful tool for addressing social and emotional issues, namely those issues pertaining to race and culture" (p. 197). Boys and young men of color should be encouraged and provided opportunities to critically reflect on stereotypes, assumptions, perspectives, and actions. This includes interrogating what they believe, as well as the perceived beliefs of those with whom they interact. In particular, boys of color should be aided in critiquing their own ethnic-male, cultural worldview and, specifically, to become more fully aware of how they see themselves in the world. Moreover, they should also be encouraged to apply a critical lens to understand economic, social, political, and racial disparities in wider society. The goal of critical reflection is to enable students to deconstruct their worlds in ways that allow them to gain a greater sense of agency and control over their own lives.

Two primary strategies for fostering critical reflection were offered by the exemplar teachers. First, teachers recommended journaling, where students write down their perceptions, emotions, and thinking about their experiences and the world in a log. Teachers suggested using journaling as a strategy for students to critically reflect on course material and organize their thoughts. One California teacher who regularly used this approach, noted that it "helped them [students] organize their thoughts in written form and helped to build confidence."

Second, teachers' overwhelmingly discussed the importance of a Socratic method in teaching boys and young men of color. In this approach, teachers use questioning to guide students in the development of and interrogation of ideas. According to a California teacher, "Socratic [methods] invite deep reflection and dialogue, helping students see they have ideas that matter." Moreover, as noted by a Texas teacher "allow for more freedom of questioning, chase every rabbit that comes up in that questioning. Questions always lead to more questions which equal learning." To support a Socratic environment, exemplar teachers recommended that students be allowed to freely express themselves, be given ample time to think critically, accept all responses (even succinct ones), and create a low-risk atmosphere for responses.

Cooperative and Collaborative Learning

Exemplar teachers discussed the importance of using cooperative learning and collaborative learning strategies for boys and young men of color. Both of these strategies entail guided learning through work in small groups via the completion of tasks. It is outside the purpose of this volume to explicate the many nuances between cooperative and collaborative learning in detail. However, in short, cooperative learning activities are typically more teacher directed, structured, closed-ended, and narrowly tailored while collaborative learning is more teacher facilitated, fluid, and open-ended. As such, cooperative learning is best employed when teaching foundational knowledge while collaborative learning is best for facilitating socially constructed knowledge (McInnereny & Roberts, 2004; Rockwood, 1995a, 1995b).

Teachers addressed the futility of lecture-style (e.g., chalk and talk, stand and deliver) approaches to learning. One California teacher stated, "another teaching strategy that I employ that I think is unique to helping young boys of color is to stay away from direct instruction as much as possible…I attempt to have student centered and student led cooperative groups where students construct their own knowledge. For students of color, this allows for both cultural expression and connection to knowledge in a way that is meaningful to them, rather than from a teacher who lives an experience vastly different from them." A number of different strategies for small group learning was discussed by educators, including: group investigation, group discussions, case studies, problem-based learning, simulations, and peer tutoring. However, the exemplar teachers seemed to favor small group designs where children were responsible for teaching one another.

The exemplary teachers seemed to favor small group designs where children were responsible for teaching one another.

Exemplar teachers discussed a number benefits for small group learning designs. They noted that these designs allow students to speak freely, experience team-work and interactions with others, learn about the assets they bring to the learning experience, have a safe learning environment, increase their confidence and self-esteem, and (for collaborative learning) to negotiate critical life moments. For instance, another California teacher stated "small group discussions. This was important because it was a way to get the boys to think about things they had seen and experienced and discuss how to work through tough situations."

Engage Problem (Project)-Based Learning

Many teachers in this study discussed the importance of problem-based learning, as well as the subcategories of inquiry-based and project-based learning. Problem-based learning represents a family of teaching strategies that "teach inquiry and problem-solving skills, content, and self-derived learning developments" and "as its name implies, uses a problem as a focal point for student investigation and inquiry" (Jacobsen et al., 2002, p. 206). Problem-based learning has several distinguishing elements, including: a) students begin their learning with a problem or question; b) students are responsible for solving the problem or question; and c) the teacher facilitates their problem-solving activities (Jacobsen et al., 2002).

Projects should focus on addressing real-world issues relevant to their lives.

Among the subcategories of this learning approach, project-based learning was repeatedly emphasized. In the vein of project-based learning, (a type of problem-based learning), a similar approach is taken, except that the project is the focus of the inquiry. In project-based learning, the end goal is a presentation or tangible product that demonstrates cumulative learning. As noted by a Texas teacher, educators must prioritize "Project-based learning [as] young men of color, as most students, need learning episodes that are practical to solving real world problems." Thus, projects should focus on addressing real-world issues relevant to their lives. Similarly, a New York teacher stated "project-based learning is an amazing way to engage students. Allowing young people to choose their paths for research and learning turns kids on! Instead of saying, 'We will be learning about this,' we say, 'What do you want to know more about and how do you want to learn it?' Of course, this is only a benefit for problem-based learning when teachers focus the problems on real-world issues that students face.

Teachers in this study noted that project-based learning allowed for greater levels of creativity, engagement, interaction, and interest. Moreover, research has shown that problem-based learning strategies allow students to "learn to regulate and control their own learning" (Jacobsen et al., 2002, p. 207). Obviously, for boys in general (and boys of color in particular) having a sense of control in academic learning environments is key to socialized desires for self-reliance and control. Moreover, this learning strategy often involves interactivity, a key component for allowing the types of movement that better support male learning patterns.

Foster Healthy Competition

Sex differences and gender socialization processes foster competition among boys. Given this, many educators recommended tapping into these inclinations to promote learning. Specifically, exemplar teachers noted the importance of implementing activities in the classroom that foster healthy competition among students. As noted by a New York teacher, "I am always talking about the boys and how great we are. I set up competitive situations in my daily classroom instruction. Boys, I believe, love competition." Competition can be integrated into the classroom through games that address multiple areas of learning and development. For instance, one Texas teacher encouraged educators to employ the "Use of competition. Boys in general, but boys of color tend to thrive in situations where they can compete against one another. The competitions may be academic, behavioral, character based, etc., but when the students think it's a game, they align themselves more readily and have a greater eagerness to participate."

Healthy competition can have many benefits in classroom environments. According to the exemplar teachers, competition encourages participation, a desire to succeed, and fosters a greater sense of belonging in school. Bearing this in mind, one Georgia teacher talked about the benefits for engagement saying, "I also play review games that allow for competition. Boys love to compete and are willing to stay engaged when they know their team must win." In addressing the benefit for boys of color, a New York teacher stated "I set up competitive situations in my daily classroom instruction. Elementary is a female dominated profession. Many kids come from single parent homes. When we highlight the boys it give them a special sense of being."

Leadership Opportunities

Provide them with opportunities to be 'center stage' in an environment where they are usually 'back stage.'

Many of the educators in this study noted that the traditional curriculum, methods of teaching, and schooling processes are exclusionary to boys and young men of color, which can result in them feeling a sense of isolation and alienation in school, and a perception that school is not for them. Teachers stated that these perceptions are reinforced by stereotypes of these men as unintelligent. As a result, teachers extolled the importance of re-centering the power structure in the classroom. Specifically, they recommended providing regular opportunities for Black and Latino males to serve as classroom leaders. This could include leadership on projects, small group discussions, large group discussions, and debates. For instance, one California teacher stated "another strategy is to choose students of color to have leadership positions in the classroom on a rotating basis, whether it is leading discussion groups, being a recorder for class discussions, or asking their opinion about conducting a particular activity. I believe that all students want to feel as if they have a voice in the classroom, but especially students of color." Beyond these recommendations, some teachers even recommended having males of color serve as the class representative or spokesperson to the teacher.

The main focus of this strategy is to provide them with opportunities to be *center stage* in an environment where they are usually *backstage*. As noted by a California teacher, this strategy can be critical to student success, "running an engaging classroom is important. Holding high expectations for behavior is important for all students. But, allowing boys of color to take center stage in a positive way (debates, shout outs, etc.) goes a long way." Another California teacher stated that this strategy provided a platform for boys of color to better rise to the task (i.e., reach high expectations). This teacher noted the value of leadership strategies, saying, "Providing leadership where students of color serve in leadership roles with projects. They rise to the task at hand and do amazing work compared to when they are not in leadership roles" suggesting that this strategy led to numerous benefits, including increased self-confidence, higher levels of engagement, a greater sense of belonging in school, and a higher quality of work.

In all, the recommended teaching and learning strategies (e.g., culturally relevant content, addressing racism and stereotypes, mastery learning, critical reflection, cooperative and collaborative learning, problem or project-based learning, healthy competition, and leadership opportunities) can serve to improve outcomes for boys and young men of color in education. As noted throughout this volume, these strategies are not necessarily unique to Black and Latino males, rather they can serve to benefit all students. However, as described by exemplar teachers, these strategies have an intensified effect on the success of males of color. The next chapter explores additional strategies that are useful for boys of color, focusing specifically on assets (through the lens of multiple intelligences) that can also be leveraged in classroom learning.

REFERENCES

Howard, T. C. (2003). Culturally relevant pedagogy: Ingredients for critical teacher reflection. *Theory into Practice, 42*(3), 195-202.

Jacobsen, D. A., Eggen, P., & Kauchak, D. (2002). *Methods for teaching: Promoting student learning.* Upper Saddle River, NJ: Merrill-Prentice Hall.

Ladson-Billings, G. (1992). Liberatory consequences of literacy: A case of culturally relevant instruction for African American students. *The Journal of Negro Education, 61,* 378-391.

McInnerney, J. M., & Roberts, T. S. (2004). Collaborative or cooperative learning? In T. S. Roberts (Ed), *Online collaborative learning: Theory and practice* (pp.203-214). London, UK: Information Science.

Rockwood, H. S. III (1995a). Cooperative and collaborative learning. *The National Teaching & Learning Forum, 4*(6), 8-9.

Rockwood, H. S. III (1995b). Cooperative and collaborative learning. *The National Teaching & Learning Forum, 5*(1), 8-10.

Wood, J. L., Harris III, F., & White, K. (2015). *Teaching men of color in the community college: A guidebook.* San Diego, CA: Montezuma.

CHAPTER 6

Differentiation and Multiple Intelligences

This chapter will address pedagogical strategies that emerged from the exemplar teacher study that addressed the importance of differentiation in the classroom. This chapter focuses on differentiation strategies that can be employed by leveraging multiple intelligences (assets) commonly held by boys and young men of color.

In recognizing that students from all racial and gender groups learn differently, differentiated instruction was recommended as a strategy for teaching boys and young men of color. Differentiation is an instructional planning and implementation method where educators attend to the diverse needs, interests, learning styles, and abilities of their students (Gregory, 2008; Gregory & Chapman, 2007; Tomlinson, 1999). According to a California teacher, differentiated instruction is important for boys of color because "all students have different needs, so it is imperative to meet the child where he is in order to help him reach his zone of proximal development and full potential to have success in a society that has stacked the odds against him."

Differentiation is an instructional planning and implementation method where educators attend to the diverse needs, interests, learning styles, and abilities of their student.

According to the exemplar teachers, educators using a differentiated approach should: a) have an understanding of the learners' learning styles, multiple intelligences, and areas for improvement; b) assess the learner in the intended area of growth; c) create different strategies for teaching lessons that can leverage varied learning styles and intelligences; d) implement different instructional strategies with a focus on individualized learner needs; and e) evaluate growth and areas for additional knowledge development. Tomlinson (2000) noted that differentiation focuses on employing varied content, processes, products, and environments. These represent four areas where differentiation can occur. Specifically, *content* refers to using materials that address different ability levels, learning styles, and supplemental instruction to enhance learners' knowledge. *Process* entails the manner in which the material is taught, through tiered activities, individualized learner plans, and time on task variation. *Products* are the tangible materials produced by students and used by educators to assess learning. And finally, the learning *environment* refers to variations in physical locales, noise, lighting, and climate of support. In general, comments from exemplar teachers focused on the content (and process to a lesser degree) that should be used in the classroom. Primarily, their comments centered on styles of learning and intelligences.

Learning Styles and Multiple Intelligences

There are great differences in the challenges, assets, experiences, and needs of boys of color. They are not one monolithic group, rather they are the same...but different.

One strategy for meeting the needs of diverse learners is to be attentive to differences in learning styles, this is important because there are great differences in the challenges, assets, experiences, and needs of boys of color. They are not one monolithic group, rather they are the same (in terms of a shared racial ancestry and sex), but different. In discussing the importance of leveraging different learning styles, one California teacher stated, "my experience is more involved with working with boys who are Latino. I work for the district's mentor program. All of my young men are English language learners to some degree, and I find that I need to use multiple styles to effectively advance their reading comprehension."

As noted by Denig (2004), there are several physiological-perceptual learning styles. They include auditory learners (those who learn best by hearing and listening); visual learners (those who learn best by seeing and reading); tactile learners (those who prefer to learn by manipulating items with their hands); and kinesthetic learners (those who learn most effectively through movement and active participation). Individuals often have learning styles that represent a nexus of multiple styles. For instance, some students may be both hands-on (tactile) and active learners (kinesthetic), referred to as tactile/kinesthetic learning or kinesthetic/tactile learners, depending upon which style is most dominant.

Individuals often have learning styles that represent a nexus of multiple styles.

62

Learning styles are a function of which sense (e.g., touch, hearing, seeing) is activated when the learning is taking place. This notion has been criticized for being overly simplistic, as the sense activated does not necessarily mean that the same cognitive faculties are used. As noted by Howard Gardner (2013), "the implication is that some people learn through their eyes, others through their ears. This notion is incoherent. Both spatial information and reading occur with the eyes, but they make use of entirely different cognitive faculties. Similarly, both music and speaking activate the ears, but again these are entirely different cognitive faculties. Recognizing this fact, the concept of intelligences does not focus on how linguistic or spatial information reaches the brain—via eyes, ears, hands, it doesn't matter. What matters is the power of the mental computer, the intelligence that acts upon that sensory information, once picked up" (para. 3).

Gardner's (1995) work on multiple intelligences presents an alternative way for understanding individuals' assets by focusing on the cognitive faculties that are employed by learners. Stated more simply, learning styles focus on the senses used and how they support a student's learning, whereas multiple intelligences focus on the cognitive faculties used and how these faculties represent individuals' assets (or intelligences). Gardner initially explicated seven intelligences (though he later added naturalist intelligence). They include the following:

- Logical-mathematic – Sensitivity to, and capacity to discern, logical or numerical patterns; ability to handle long chains of reasoning.
- Linguistic- Sensitivity to the sounds, rhythms, and meanings of words; sensitivity to the different functions of language.
- Musical – Abilities to produce and appreciate rhythm, pitch, and timbre; appreciation of the forms of music expressiveness.
- Spatial – Capacities to perceive the visual-spatial world accurately and to perform transformations on one's initial perceptions.
- Bodily-Kinesthetic – Abilities to control one's body movements and to handle objects skillfully.
- Interpersonal – Capacities to discern and respond appropriately to the moods, temperaments, motivations, and desires of other people.
- Intrapersonal – Access to one's own feelings and the ability to discriminate among them and draw upon them to guide behavior; knowledge of one's own strengths, weaknesses, desires, and intelligences (Gardner & Hatch, 1989, p. 6).

We focus on multiple intelligences because it is an asset-based lens for viewing the strengths that boys and young men of color bring into the classroom.

Differentiated instruction should levy the use of all learning styles and multiple intelligences to support the success of Black and Latino males; however, exemplar teachers repeatedly noted that boys of color seem to learn best through certain styles and intelligences. Using the lens of multiple intelligences, we present several areas that exemplar teachers highlighted as being critical for supporting the education of males of color. However, three key points should be noted. First, educators did not make distinctions between learning styles and intelligences. Though they are distinct concepts, we present aggregated themes for these areas in tandem through the lens of multiple intelligences. Second, we focus on multiple intelligences because it is an asset-based lens for viewing the strengths that boys and young men of color bring into the classroom. Third, while Black and Latino males (either by socialization, expectation, or function of the brain) may learn better using one approach or another, it is critical that they gain exposure to all learning styles and have opportunities to develop intelligences in all areas. Doing so is key to their long-term success.

As an overarching theme, educators made it clear that boys and young men of color learned most effectively when their visual-spatial, musical-rhythmic, bodily-kinesthetic, and linguistic-verbal intelligences were leveraged. Often, teachers talked about activating intelligences in more than one area simultaneously. For example, a Florida teacher stated that boys of color must have a "visual presentation of material and interactive strategies." Teachers made similar statements about music and movement. Overwhelmingly, teachers argued that auditory learning should not be prioritized. For example, a California teacher stated that educators must "Model with manipulatives. This is important because a lot of young boys of color process information using their visual and kinesthetic abilities versus auditory abilities. This strategy allows for boys to incorporate language and physicality while giving them visual pictures of what is being taught."

Visual-Spatial Intelligence

Exemplar teachers repeatedly noted the importance of using visual aids. They remarked that educators should use visual presentations that have pictures and graphics that connect directly to the daily lives and experiences of boys of color. As noted by a Florida teacher, "the visual presentation strategy supports the written material which boys of color can find daunting [and] builds connections to the material." Similarly, a California teacher noted that they used "video game type quizzes and/or activities *with graphics* that they can relate to and make a connection" which seemed to engage boys during lessons. In like manner, a Texas teacher stated "[I use] Strategy Art...Using art in my lessons provides men of color an opportunity to demonstrate thoughts that perhaps they do not have the language for to express orally." Specifically, exemplar teachers recommended the use of pictures, charts, graphs, maps, movies, video clips, and art.

According to Gregory and Chapman (2007), there are a number of strategies that can be used to leverage visual-spatial intelligence. Some examples include having students draw pictures, diagram key events, color, create displays, draft cartoons, develop photo essays, sculpture, and make posters. These are some among many other strategies that may work for boys and young men of color. As noted in Chapter 2, boys' brains may be best stimulated by visual aids. So, this recommendation falls in line with that research. Of course, key to the success of these strategies will be ensuring that the visual aids themselves (used for teaching materials) and visual-spatial abilities activated by classroom activities are culturally relevant to the lived realities of Black and Latino males.

Musical-Rhythmic Intelligence

Musical-rhythmic activities maintain high levels of engagement, allow for expression, exerts natural energies, and supports focus on academics.

A number of teachers addressed the importance of leveraging musical-rhythmic intelligence with students. As noted earlier, this type of intelligence deals with both the production and appreciation of music. Teachers recommended leveraging this asset through chanting, music, and dancing. With respect to the latter, dancing has often been cross-listed as a bodily-kinesthetic intelligence, and we present it here because the exemplar teachers connected dancing itself to music. Teachers in this study noted that musical-rhythmic activities were beneficial, as the integration of music maintains high levels of engagement, allows for expression, exerts natural energies, and supports a focus on academics. As noted by a teacher from Georgia, "we do a lot of moving, crazy dancing, and silly songs with boys." Thus, music simply makes learning more enjoyable. Moreover, music better enables students to learn and remember new concepts (i.e., knowledge retention). As noted by two California teachers, educators must engage "Movement and song or music. Young boys love to move and be active. Music is such an integral part of African American culture, it is all around us. Music and song help to aid memory and it makes learning fun and accessible. It is a great way to teach unfamiliar vocabulary and concepts" and "honor the best of their music and lifestyles. Give them real opportunities to sing, chant and dance as they learn new concepts in Language Arts, Math, Social Studies or Science." Similarly, a Texas teacher noted that they use music as a strategy as it is "engaging and seems to provide successful achievement of the [class] content for boys of color."

Bodily-Kinesthetic Intelligence

Hands on activities with movement emerged from this study as *the* most recurrent theme across all themes. Specifically, exemplar teachers strongly recommended activity-based learning as the primary first-step strategy for enhancing the learning experiences of boys of color. This educational strategy was perceived as activating tactile-kinesthetic learning styles as well as leveraging the assets of bodily-kinesthetic intelligence. As noted by a teacher from California, educators must "accept, plan for, and adapt curriculum and discipline practices to fit the energy that male students of color bring to the classroom." Teachers noted that planning for this energy is important for all boys, but in particular for boys of color, as their movements and activity are more likely to be pathologized. In making this point, several teachers expressed that the energy of boys of color is natural, not an attention, hyperactive, or emotional disorder. As noted by teachers from Florida and California, "Kinesthetic learning gives boys more hands on work and gets them moving" and "many boys of color learn by doing... They need many hands-on experiences that incorporate movement and opportunities to experiment with guided practice that is encouraging and complimentary."

Exemplar teachers strongly recommended activity-based learning as the primary first-step strategy for enhancing the learning experiences of boys of color. This educational strategy was perceived as activating tactile-kinesthetic learning styles as well as leveraging the assets of bodily-kinesthetic intelligence.

Exemplar teachers noted numerous benefits for using movement coupled with hands-on activities in class. This included: reducing relational distractions, increasing engagement, dispelling boredom, livening up the classroom, and making learning enjoyable. As one Georgia teacher stated, "when we are moving, we are learning! I love to find games and activities that get us out of our seats! Boys seem to really enjoy having the opportunity to get up and move. This is one of my favorite times to look for those teachable moments." Moreover, a teacher from California commented that movement is critical to classroom focus, stating "I have a lot of movement in my classroom. All kids benefit from stretching to focus, and my experience shows me that boys benefit from having a chance to energize and wiggle." In all this teacher and others noted that activity-based learning helps to maintain class control by allowing boys (in general) and boys of color (in particular) to exert necessary energies.

Teachers from the study discussed a number of ideas for engaging movement and hands-on activity in the classroom. They remarked that using this approach could be as simple as allowing students to stand, having a short exercise before an activity, or allowing students to do sound and body movements during reading. Many educators also talked about the integration of athletic activities, physical games, and video games as key strategies. A number of other strategies were recommended by exemplar teachers, here are some selected examples:

- *Objects for Math.* Using hands-on activities with airplanes and video games to address math word problems.
- *Role Playing.* Using role-playing and classroom theater to teach concepts (this allows for a physical experience while learning and can build confidence).
- *Quiz Bowls.* Creating a quiz bowl for students to compete while demonstrating knowledge attainment.

Two in-depth examples were discussed by teachers from Texas. One teacher stated, "I plan lessons that have movement in them (building a cave having the students get up, explore the cave, write conclusions in groups about the artifacts they found in the cave) punctuated with times of mental focus." Touching on the importance of integrating tactile and kinesthetic activities, another teacher stated: "at one campus of all boys I work with (…offenders, adjudicated, and drug treatment), we are building an obstacle course. We use math, reading, and the physical act of building. Then we plan to use the course in classes to stimulate the brain with movement. Students must complete an obstacle and solve a problem in varying contents to move on to the next."

Linguistic-Oral Intelligence

According to Gardner and Hatch (1989), linguistic intelligence involves students' "sensitivity to the sounds, rhythms, and meanings of words; sensitivity to the different functions of language." This intelligence is usually associated with verbal, written, and reading strengths. Our findings around linguistic intelligence suggest a departure from Gardner's frame. Specifically, exemplar teachers discussed the linguistic intelligence of boys and young men of color; however, these assets were perceived as being most dominant in oral communication (as opposed to reading and writing). We refer to this here as linguistic-oral intelligence to be more specific about the oral assets of boys and young men of color. According to Boykin (1994), this relates directly to cultural characteristics and assets that students of color have that are rooted in an oral tradition. More specifically, Ford, Harris III, Tyson, and Trotman (2002) noted that students of color have "strong preference for oral modes of communication; students speak frankly, directly, and honestly; students enjoy playing with language (puns, jokes, innuendoes, storytelling, etc)" (p. 54).

For communities of color, oral histories, stories, and language are a core aspect of culture and cultural transmission.

It is not uncommon for boys of color to excel at verbal communication and have more difficulties with written communication. As noted by a California teacher, "many children of color come from homes that are far more focused on the spoken word than on the written word (either due to not being proficient in English, perhaps not having completed school themselves, or to simply being in a culture that is very oral)." With respect to the latter point, for communities of color, oral histories, stories, and language are a core aspect of culture and cultural transmission. As a result, teachers who require students to demonstrate knowledge attainment solely through writing may conclude that students know less about a topic than they actually do. Teachers repeatedly extolled the importance of allowing males of color to orally process information and demonstrate knowledge attainment orally.

This notion is affirmed by statements from two California teachers who said, "Boys of color often make sense of content through discussion" and "Some boys, I have found, prefer to type and/or orally share responses on various assignments rather than take copious notes." Similarly, another California teacher stated they "Incorporated verbal and aural responses as valid indicators of concept comprehension." In like manner, a Texas teacher noted "African American boys of color have excellent verbal skills... so I allow them to use their creativity with words based on projects that I assign and getting them to participate in debate." For young men of color, other exemplar teachers encouraged the use of debate to demonstrate learning mastery. A Texas teacher stated, "Debate. This is a good strategy to foster metacognition while allowing students to vocalize their own understanding of a particular concept. This allows students to be passionate in defense of their argument or position."

One common oral processing strategy recommended by exemplar teachers was call and response. Call and response is a common cultural communication pattern for communities of color, particularly African American communities. In this communication pattern, an individual calls out with a statement or question and other individuals respond with a prescribed response. In the African American church, two common examples of this include:

Example 1: Preacher: God is good → Congregation: All the time
Preacher: All the time → Congregation: God is good

Example 2: Preacher: Can I get an Amen? → Congregation: Amen!

A number of exemplar teachers discussed using call and response to engage students in the learning process. For example, two California teachers said the following: "The communities where these young men come from are communities who are very verbal. Call and response is common" and "I use a lot of call and response. Kids are encouraged to join in. As with all good teaching moves this is good for all of my kids, but/and it resonates with kids of color for whom this mode might be familiar from home and church." In the classroom, teachers can employ rhythmic or fun chant-like responses to course material to help structure learning. This is an area where linguistic-oral intelligence may converge with music-rhythmic intelligence. Given the predominance of call and response in communication and music, students will likely recognize the patterns, thereby making school feel more familiar and exciting.

Teachers should also recognize that a large segment of Black and Latino males may have home languages and dialects (e.g., ebony-phonics, Spanglish, Spanish, Portuguese) that differ from that of their school language. These languages are assets to the learning experience for boys and young men of color. They serve as a resource that can be tapped into to help students make connections between concepts. That being said, students may need assistance in switching back and forth between languages, with reminders about what classroom voice looks like in comparison to home voice. Some teachers noted that this may require initial ground work to provide a necessary foundation in school language to support leveraging activities. For instance, one California teacher stated, "Many of my boys of color are English language learners, which requires topic specific and academic vocabulary to be front loaded."

A dichotomy should not be created between home language and school language that prioritizes one; rather, educators should embrace both methods of oral communication.

Notwithstanding, a dichotomy should not be created between home language and school language that prioritizes one; rather, educators should embrace both methods of oral communication. One Florida teacher noted, "I try to explain how formal language can be broken down into their own vernacular language. I can laugh at myself while they laugh at me." Similarly, a teacher from New York stated "I OPENLY teach code switching, "the way to be in school," we talk about what life and study skills we need to succeed." Exemplar teachers noted the numerous benefits of leveraging home language through teaching code switching. These benefits included: build bonds with students, facilitate early learning and success, make connections between home cultures and in-class learning, and support language acquisition.

REFERENCES

Boykin, A. W. (1994). Afrocultural expression and its implications for schooling. In E. R. Hollins, J. E. King, & W. C. Hayman (Eds.), *Teaching diverse populations: Formulating a knowledge base* (pp.225-273). New York, NY: State University of New York.

Denig, S. J. (2004). Multiple intelligences and learning styles: Two complementary dimensions. *Teachers College Record, 106*(1), 96-111.

Ford, D. Y, Harris III, J. J., Tyson, C. A., & Trotman, M. F. (2002). Beyond deficit thinking: Providing access for gifted African American students. *Roeper Review, 24*(2), 52-58.

Gardner, H. (1995). Reflections on multiple intelligences: Myths and messages. *Phi Delta Kappan, 77*, 200-209.

Gardner, H. (2013, October 16). Howard Gardner: 'Multiple intelligences' are not 'learning styles.' Interview conducted by Valerie Strauss. *Washington Post.*

Gardner, H., & Hatch, T. (1989). Multiple intelligences go to school: Educational implications of the theory of multiple intelligences. *Educational Researcher, 18*(8), 4-10.

Gregory, G. H. (2008). *Differentiated instructional strategies in practice: Training, implementation, and supervision.* Thousand Oaks, CA: Corwin.

Gregory, G. H., & Chapman, C. (2007). *Differentiated instructional strategies: One size does not fit all.* Thousand Oaks, CA: Corwin.

Tomlinson, C. (1999). Mapping a route toward differentiated instruction. *Educational Leadership, 57*(1), 12-16.

Tomlinson, C. A. (2000). Differentiation of instruction in the elementary grades (ED443572). *ERIC clearinghouse on elementary and early childhood education.* Champaign, IL: ERIC Digests.

CHAPTER 7

Classroom Management

This chapter discusses classroom management strategies and practices offered by exemplar teachers. These practices touch upon proactive approaches to reducing disciplinary issues as well as strategies for handling disciplinary concerns as they arise.

Classroom management is often a critical concern for educators. Communicating curricular content to students can be impeded when teachers do not have control of their classrooms. As previously noted, boys and young men of color are often exposed to exclusionary discipline that removes them from classroom through suspensions or expulsions. Often, this is a byproduct of teachers' desire to maintain classroom control, a feeling that is often unduly heightened when educating Black and Latino males. According to UCLA Professor Tyrone Howard, schools must eliminate "punitive policies such as Zero Tolerance, which has led to a grossly disproportionate number of suspensions and expulsions of boys of color" (Howard, 2014, para. 10). Exemplar teachers offered strategies that educators could use to support classroom management. These practices addressed proactive approaches for reducing disciplinary issues, as well as strategies for handling disciplinary concerns as they occur.

Teachers' desire to maintain classroom control, a feeling that is often unduly heightened when educating Black and Latino males.

Reject Socially Constructed Deficits and Fears

As addressed extensively in this volume, the actions of boys and young men of color are often pathologized. This results in them being viewed as deviants and delinquents by educators. As such, these males are suspended and expelled at much higher rates than their peers. Moreover, pathologized views have resulted in the significant overrepresentation of Black and Latino males in special education as emotionally disturbed. It is important to note, as discussed previously, that having an anti-deficit view of boys and young men of color is an essential foundation undergirding meaningful practices with them. Specifically, a California teacher stated the following: "As the instructor, you have to be firm and fair. Sometimes teachers tend to fear African American young men. In the spirit of total honesty. Everyone knows that African Americans come in all colors. It often seems that the darker the pigment the more feared they are by their teachers, particularly younger female teachers. These young men have 3 strikes against them when they walk into class the first time. 1) They are male; 2) they are dark skinned; and 3) they are tall. A six foot 8th or 9th grader (or any student under 16 for that matter) can appear to be intimidating. But they shouldn't be feared. You can't teach someone you're afraid of. If he pops out of the seat and starts roaming around class, ask (or even tell) him to sit down, and remind him of the class rules. It may take time, after time, after time but he'll eventually get the message." While this example focuses on African American males, similar perceptions of fear may often be held about Latino males. We reiterate the point made by this teacher "You can't teach someone you're afraid of." A teacher who conveys fear also communicates to the student that they do not matter and do not belong. Such messages inhibit any progress in building meaningful relationships with students that can foster student success.

Employ Fair Disciplinary Practices

Employ fair and consistent disciplinary practices that don't treat boys' actions differently due to race.

Educators must enact proactive measures for successful classroom management. However, the desire to be more restrictive with boys of color than their peers is rooted in a stereotypical perspective of them as criminals and deviants. These perceptions are socialized in the minds of *all* educators. As such, a critical point noted by many teachers in this study was the need to employ fair and consistent disciplinary practices that don't treat boys' actions differently due to race. In earlier chapters, we highlighted research that noted that the actions of boys of color can be pathologized, even when those same actions are displayed by other boys. Moreover, when actions are viewed as equivalent between males of color and their peers, they are more likely to be subject to harsher discipline. This falls in line with an anxious desire to maintain control, often when actions are already in control. In this light, a New York teacher stated, "I am extremely mindful of not disciplining boys and young men of color any differently from my other students. Again, I believe this is something to which they have become accustomed, and it is so important to me to negate that pattern in my classroom." Negating this pattern requires that teachers be consciously aware of their actions. Often, this may include reflection upon disciplinary practices in action as well as at the days' end. Teachers must consider whether the actions that prompted discipline were different than other boys and whether they were responded to with harsher punishments for boys of color. Reflective practice is key to employing fair disciplinary practices.

Maintain Clear and Consistent Expectations

Consistency provides a necessary framework for structure and a sense of control in the environment.

It is also critical that teachers are consistent with their standards in the classroom. Teachers must maintain the standards that they set forth in class. Students respond to both standards set forth by educators and actions that reinforce those standards. Thus, classroom rules in place should be consistently reinforced by the teacher. As such, if there is a policy about raising one's hand to leave their seat, then the policy should be enforced consistently. When a teacher ignores the policy, it can send mixed messages to students and lead them to perceive that the policy as unimportant. Teachers noted that consistency provides a necessary framework for structure and a sense of control in the environment. Moreover, expectations must be clearly communicated to students. As noted by a New York teacher "Communication with the student and establishing an understanding of expectations [is critical]. The students need to understand what is expected." In addition to being clear about rules and policies, teachers must also be clear about the consequences of not adhering to expectations. According to a Texas teacher "laying out the expectations and consequences for not meeting them" is essential to the success of boys and young men of color. In cases where it is necessary to deviate from expectations, it is critical that the teacher communicate this to students in order to acknowledge the deviation and provide a rationale for its occurrence. As stated by a California teacher "You MUST BE 100% consistent in everything: strategies discipline, technique, etc. If you deviate from that you, should let them know why it has happened."

Consider Using Directives

Researchers have long used Baumrind's (1991) taxonomy of parenting styles to better understand how discipline practices vary across race, ethnicity, and culture. Baumrind argued that there were four primary parenting approaches, including authoritarian, authoritative, permissive, and neglecting-rejecting. *Authoritarian* parenting places a higher emphasis on demanding actions and low in responsiveness. More simply, authoritarian parents are domineering and autocratic while also inhibiting two-way communication between the child and parent. *Authoritative* parenting places a higher emphasis both on demanding actions and in responsiveness. As such, this style (while still controlling of behavior) allows for two-way communication between the child and parent regarding decision-making, rules, and family plans. *Permissive* parenting places a lower emphasis on demands and higher emphasis on responsiveness. As such, this style allows children to have freedom in decision-making while also having few rules for them to follow. Finally, *neglecting-rejecting* parenting places both low demands on children and is unresponsive to them, in essence, lacking a clearly formed structure for behavior.

Extensive research has shown that White middle-class families are more likely to employ authoritative parenting (Darling, 1999; Rudasill, Adelson, Callahan, Houlihan and Keizer, 2013) while Black and Latino families are more likely to be authoritarian (Arredondo et al., 2006; Lamborn, Dornbusch, & Steinberg, 1996). Parenting styles can influence children's responsiveness to teachers in the classroom. Making the connection between disciplinary structures in the home and the misalignment of those structures in school, exemplar teachers recommended that educators be more directive (commonly associated with authoritarian styles). We present this finding with ambivalence, as there are weaknesses associated with directives. Chief among those weaknesses is not allowing space for dialogue, an approach that limits the development of necessary critical-analytic skills. Moreover, parenting styles represent generalities among groups as parents of all races use all styles and their interpretations of these styles are vastly different (see Mandara, 2006).

Parenting styles represent generalities among groups as parents of all races use all styles and their interpretations of these styles are vastly different.

Thus, we would rather communicate that, for *some* Black and Latino males directives *may* be a good initial approach to mirroring disciplinary practices that they *may* experience at home. With this perspective in mind, a California teacher stated, "I am very direct in giving instructions. I don't ask, I tell. Nicely, but firmly. I think this is important for all students but I think the directness is effective with boys of color because it is more in line with what they would have heard at home." Similarly, another California teacher noted "I am direct. I do not say, 'Would you like to go to your seat?' I say, 'Please go to your seat.' But I use a calm neutral tone and try my best to remember the '*please*.' I keep a calm tone and don't engage, because if I get angry, they get angry and shut down." Finally, echoing these comments, a Georgia teacher commented, "with boys you must be matter of fact. My students know my expectations and they are very clear. I do not allow any "questioning" or "what if" discussions to occur. I give the directions with examples and we get bye. I think boys need the "here it is, do it" strategy."

Allow Time for Brain Breaks

As noted earlier in this book, it is not uncommon for students to become over stimulated when there is substantial activity in the classroom. In particular, switching between many tasks can lead to frustration. Frustration is often combined with anger and aggression (as they occur in the same brain center). Moreover, we also highlighted research that demonstrated the need for boys to engage a *rest state* in shifting between activities. This rest state serves to recharge the brain before entering into new activities (but is often interpreted as disengagement and zoning out). Informed by practical experience, teachers in this study recommended that boys be provided with short brain breaks between exercises. As noted by a Georgia teacher, I recommend "spacing assignments in order to give them time... This is important for boys and young men of color in order for them to be successful and not get bored. They seem to be more attentive with spacing of assignments. Also brain breaks work well with boys and young men of color." The teachers did not recommend a specific time period between assignments for brain breaks, the amount of time will likely differ by the age and maturity of the student. However, being attentive to the need for short breaks when transitioning between topics was recommended.

Employ Strategies to Refocus Attention

Boys and young men of color…are often exposed to high levels of stressful life events that can distract from their directed attention on academic matters.

Students may be distracted after a brain break, recess, lunch, or upon arriving to school. When returning to the class physically or mentally, it is important to refocus students' attention. By refocusing attention, we are referring to strategies that help to transition students back into a time of learning. This is critically important, particularly for boys and young men of color who are often exposed to high levels of stressful life events that can distract from their directed attention on academic matters. As noted by a New York teacher, "Refocusing and redirection is important because the students often enter the classroom distracted from something that has occurred outside the class." In like manner, a Georgia teacher stated that when entering the classroom "the first strategy I use with boys and young men of color is that of making sure that attention levels are appropriate and everyone is attentive to the lesson being taught." Exemplar teachers did not recommend specific strategies for regaining classroom control, rather, emphasizing that refocusing attention was necessary. Likely, the strategies used will differ by age; however, we have seen teachers effectively use synchronized clapping (i.e., "if you hear my voice clap once, if you hear my voice clap twice"), raising one's finger to their mouth to indicate silence and waiting for others to respond, and the teacher speaking with a very quiet voice until students respond by lowering their tone. These strategies work when regaining students' focus. However, they may not be adequate for regaining mental focus. Some teachers recommended mindfulness practices, a quiet time of reflection, and journaling as initial ways to help regain mental focus.

Use Non-Confrontational Tones

When addressing actions that are not in line with the clear and consistent standards set forth by the teacher, it is essential that teachers use non-confrontational tones. Non-confrontational tones means that the language employed is communicated in a calm, non-hostile, respectful manner. For example, a California teacher stated, "refrain from confrontational tones and demeanor when speaking with men of color." Similarly, another California teacher stated "Always use a quiet, calm voice when correcting - but this applies to all children." Exemplar teachers noted that the body language used when conveying critique of performance also be non-confrontational. This practice is critical to ensuring that the encounter does not escalate. In cases where the teacher "loses their cool" and uses verbal and non-verbal language that is aggressive, students will often respond with aggressive posturing. The effect of confrontational tones can be particularly damaging if communicated in front of other students, as the student may feel that their reputation is in jeopardy and respond in ways to protect their integrity. Due to the socially engrained perceptions of these males as deviants, encounters that become escalated rarely end well for boys of color. Furthermore, one encounter that demonstrates a lack of respect can mar efforts made by educators to establish relationships typified by trust, mutual respect, and authentic care.

Engage Positive Reinforcements

Positive incentives are a beneficial tool for classroom management that focuses on what students should do as opposed to what they shouldn't.

In sports, it is often said that the best offense is a good defense. In the classroom the best defense is positive reinforcement. Positive reinforcement entails using positive remarks and rewards to acknowledge actions that adhere to the clear and consistent expectations of the classroom. Positive reinforcements can range from verbal praise from teachers to more tangible rewards such as gifts, food, and extra privileges (e.g., 5 minutes more recess time). A number of teachers recommended the use of positive incentive charts to support the enactment of positive classroom actions. Incentive charts allow students to earn points for "good" behavior that can, over a specified period of time, produce specific rewards for students. A New York teacher explained that they use this approach often, stating "I am very strict but I allow for many fun activities in my class. I have an incentive chart which I use minute by minute." Positive incentives are a beneficial tool for classroom management that focuses on what students should do as opposed to what they shouldn't. It is also a non-punitive approach to educating boys and young men of color that addresses necessary concerns without feeding into social stereotypes that criminalize them.

Allow for a Fresh Start

As noted earlier in this volume, research from Ladson-Billings (2011) has noted how boys of color are often viewed through a lens that fears them and subsequently tries to control their behavior. She also noted that their transition from children to adults, in the eyes of their teachers, occurs faster than other boys. Bearing this in mind, she titled her research on this topic "Boyz to men? Teaching to restore Black boys' childhood." One of the challenges in seeing boys as men is the degree of culpability associated with actions. For example, a child who makes a mistake is merely seen as a kid who is learning to behave in accordance with classroom expectations. A man who makes a mistake is perceived as knowing better and thus deserves a more rigorous punishment and is not immediately deserving of forgiveness. This latter point was noted by exemplar teachers who strongly recommended that other teachers remember that they are teaching children and youth who will make mistakes. And, like any other child who makes a mistake, Black and Latino boys are worthy of forgiveness in the form of a fresh start.

As such, when boys and young men of color engage in actions that do not conform to teachers' standards, teachers should be willing to provide them with the same type of fresh start that they would for other students. As adeptly stated by a teacher from California, "Another strategy I use is 'Each day is a new day.' Unfortunately there is a stigma that follows boys of color throughout their school careers, especially if they have had discipline issues in the past. Some students will have reputations that precede them. I tell my students that each day is a new day. What you may have done yesterday has nothing to do with how you will be treated by me today. Each day is a new opportunity to do better."

This practice aligns with actions that teach students that school can serve as a pathway to create a positive future for themselves and their families. If the focus of education is on bettering oneself, then practices should be focused on moving forward, not holding students back for actions in the past. This is not to say that an accumulation of transgressions against classroom protocol and rules should be ignored by teachers; however, prior actions and teachers' responses to those actions can serve to convince students that "they are bad." If a student sees themselves as bad, their actions can become a self-fulfilling prophecy. However, if students perceive that they have a fresh start, they can have greater hope for creating a more positive future for themselves in school.

Critique Privately, Praise Publically

Many boys and young men of color may be fearful about affirming stereotypes that legitimize illegitimate perceptions about their ability and performance. As such, it is critical that teachers provide critiques of their performance and actions in private sessions. For instance, teachers should avoid (at all costs) any public critique of boys and young men of color with respect to their academic performance in violation of classroom and school codes of conduct. As such, any concerns about their actions should take place when other students are not around.

Teachers should avoid (at all costs) any public critique of boys and young men of color with respect to their academic performance in violation of classroom and school codes of conduct.

In cases where this is not possible, the teacher should employ a non-confrontational tone and engage the student by getting down to eye level and speaking softly so only the student and the teacher know what is being said. The most important element of critiquing actions and performance in this way is ensuring that other students are unaware of the nature of the conversation. In extreme cases, where the action may result in a public classroom discussion, the teacher should ask to speak privately with student(s). Again, these approaches are important for both addressing challenges in academic performance and classroom decorum. Given that males often seek to maintain a sense of pride and control in school settings, privately critiquing them can avoid emasculation. Numerous teachers noted the importance of this strategy, and here are some selected comments:

- "Speak with individuals personally, away from the group to help them save face and lessen the risk in whole group situations" (North Carolina teacher).
- "I correct them in private and let them come up with positive solutions for the problem. Their bravado comes before everything. You never even by accident embarrass a young man of color. He will never forget it" (Florida teacher).
- "I will pull in a student who is not performing and talk quietly with them one to one. Discuss what is working and not working in the class and how we can work together towards success. Pulling the student aside, not busting them out publicly goes is important, especially for young men of color. It is about respecting them as a human being" (California teacher).

- "Public reprimand generally results in shut down, disengagement, or disrespect. Quiet reprimand and public praise work consistently" (New York teacher).

In contrast, while challenges should be critiqued privately, teachers should publicly praise performance and actions that exceed classroom expectations. This can lead to an increase in self-confidence and further promote outcomes that are desirable to the teacher. Moreover, such messaging can also benefit other students, by deconstructing negative stereotypes about boys and young men of color. One caveat here is that public praise must be task specific and authentic in nature. Undue praise and overpraising small contributions can actually produce the opposite of the intended outcome. It is not enough for the teacher to be authentic; teachers must also ensure that their comments are received and acknowledged by the student as being authentic.

This chapter has advanced ten strategies for maintaining classroom discipline that were espoused by exemplar teachers. These strategies include: reject socially constructed deficits and fears; employ fair disciplinary practices; maintain clear and consistent expectations; consider directives; allow time for brain breaks; employ strategies for refocusing attention; use non-confrontational tones; engage positive reinforcements; allow for a fresh start; and critique privately and praise publicly. Collectively, these strategies can be used to enhance classroom management and thereby advance success for males of color.

REFERENCES

Arredondo, E. M., Elder, J. P., Ayala, G. X., Campbell, N., Baquero, B., & Duerksen, S. (2006). Is parenting style related to children's healthy eating and physical activity in Latino families? *Health Education Research, 21,* 862-871.

Baumrind, D. (1973). The development of instrumental competence through socialization. In A. D. Pick (Ed.), *Minnesota symposium on child psychology* (Vol. 7, pp. 3-46). Minneapolis: University of Minnesota Press.

Darling, N. (1999). *Parenting style and its correlates* (ERIC Digest No. 427896). Champaign: ERIC Clearinghouse on Elementary and Early Childhood Education, University of Illinois.

Howard, T. C. (2014). Why we should care about boys and young men of color. *Huffington Post.*

Ladson-Billings, G. (2011). Boyz to men? Teaching to restore Black boys' childhood. *Race Ethnicity and Education, 14*(1), 7-15.

Lamborn, S. D., Dornbusch, S. M., & Steinberg, L. (1996). Ethnicity and community context as moderators of the relations between family decision making and adolescent adjustment. *Child Development, 67*, 283-301.

Mandara, J. (2006). The impact of family functioning on African American males' academic achievement: A review and clarification of empirical literature. *Teachers College Record, 108*(2), 206-223.

Rudasill, K. M., Adelson, J. L., Callahan, C. M., Houlihan, D. V., & Keizer, B. M. (2013). Gifted students' perceptions of parenting styles: Associations with cognitive ability, sex, race, and age. *Gifted Children Quarterly, 57*(1), 15-24.

Suggested Reading List

Bonner, F.A. II. (Ed.). (2014). *Building on Resilience: Models and frameworks of Black male success Across the P-20 pipeline.* Sterling, VA: Stylus Publishing.

Fergus, E., Noguera, P., & Martin, M. (2014). *Schooling for resilience: Improving the life trajectories of African American and Latino males.* Cambridge, MA: Harvard Education.

Harper, S. R., & Wood, J. L. (Eds.). (2016). *Advancing Black male student success from preschool through Ph.D.* Sterling, VA: Stylus Publishing.

Harper, S. R., & Associates. (2014). *Succeeding in the city: A report from the New York City Black and Latino male high school achievement study.* Philadelphia, PA: University of Pennsylvania, Center for the Study of Race and Equity in Education.

Howard, T. C. (2014). *Black male(d): Peril and promise in the education of African American males.* New York, NY: Teachers College Press.

Kunjufu, J. (1983). *Countering the conspiracy to destroy Black boys.* Chicago, IL: African American Images.

Ladson-Billings, G. (2011). Boyz to men? Teaching to restore Black boys' childhood. *Race Ethnicity and Education, 14*(1), 7-15.

Moore, J. L., III, & Flowers, L. A. (2012). Increasing the representation of African American males in gifted and talented programs. In S. Lewis, M. Casserly, C. Simon, R. Uzzell, & M. Palacios (Eds.), *A call for change: Providing solutions for Black male achievement* (pp. 67-81). Washington, DC: Council of Great City Schools.

Moore, J. L., III, & Lewis, C. W. (Eds.). (2014). *African American male students in PreK-12 schools: Implications for research, practice, and policy.* Bingley, UK: Emerald.

Noguera, P. A., Hurtado, A., & Fergus, E. (Eds.) (2011). *Understanding and responding to the disenfranchisement of Latino males: Invisible no more.* New York, NY: Routledge.

Polite, V. & Davis, J. E. (1999). *African American males in school and society: Policies and Practices for Effective Education.* New York, NY: Teachers College Press, Columbia University.

Ponjuan, L., Clark, M. A., & Saenz, V. B. (2012). *Boys in peril: Examining Latino boys' educational pathways and motivations towards postsecondary education.* San Antonio, TX: TG Foundation.

Sáenz, V. B., and L. Ponjuan. 2009. The Vanishing Latino Male in Higher Education. *Journal of Hispanic Higher Education, 8*(1), 54–89.

Tatum, A. W. (2005). *Teaching reading to Black adolescent males: Closing the achievement gap.* Portland, ME: Stenhouse.

Toldson, I. A. (2008). *Breaking barriers: Plotting the path to academic success for school-age African American males.* Washington, DC: Congressional Black Caucus Foundation.

Toldson, I. A., Sutton, R. M., & Fry Brown, R. L. (2012). Preventing delinquency and promoting academic success among school-age African American males. *Journal of African American Males in Education, 3*(1), 12-28.

About the Authors

J. Luke Wood, PhD, is Associate Professor in the College of Education at San Diego State University (SDSU). Dr. Wood is also Co-Director of the Minority Male Community College Collaborative (M2C3), a national research and practice center that partners with community colleges to support their capacity in advancing outcomes for men of color. Wood's research focuses on factors affecting the success of boys, young men, and men of color in education. In particular, his research examines contributors to student persistence, achievement, attainment, and transition. Dr. Wood has delivered over a 120 scholarly professional and conference presentations. Dr. Wood has authored over 100 publications, including six co-authored books, six edited books, and more than 60 peer-reviewed journal articles. His most recent books include: *Teaching men of color in the community college: A guidebook* (co-authored with Frank Harris III and Khalid White) and *Advancing Black male student success from preschool through PhD* (co-edited with Shaun R. Harper). Dr. Wood is a former recipient of the Sally Casanova Pre-Doctoral Fellowship from which he served as research fellow at Stanford University. Wood received his PhD (2010) in Educational Leadership & Policy Studies from Arizona State University (ASU). He also holds a master's degree in Higher Education Leadership with a concentration in Student Affairs and a bachelor's degree in Black History and Politics from California State University, Sacramento. Luke is a member of Alpha Phi Alpha Fraternity Incorporated.

Frank Harris III, EdD, is Associate Professor in the College of Education and Co-Director of the Minority Male Community College Collaborative (M2C3) at San Diego State University. His research is broadly focused on student development and student success in education and explores questions related to the social construction of gender and race, males and masculinities, and racial/ethnic disparities in student outcomes. In his role as co-director of M2C3, he partners with educational institutions across the United States to conduct research and design interventions to facilitate student achievement among males who have been historically marginalized in postsecondary education. Harris also regularly disseminates his scholarship through refereed conference proceedings, workshops, symposia, and keynote addresses—having delivered more than 100 academic and professional presentations since 2004. Harris earned a bachelor's degree in Communication Studies from Loyola Marymount University, a master's degree in Speech Communication from California State University Northridge, and an EdD in Higher Education from the University of Southern California - Rossier School of Education. Frank is a member of Alpha Phi Alpha Fraternity Incorporated.

www.ingramcontent.com/pod-product-compliance
Lightning Source LLC
Chambersburg PA
CBHW050843270326
41930CB00019B/3450